Library of
Davidson College

VOID

Peter Lang

Richard C. Trexler

Naked Before the Father

The Renunciation of

Francis of Assisi

Humana Civilitas 9

Published under the auspices of the
CENTER FOR MEDIEVAL AND RENAISSANCE STUDIES
University of California, Los Angeles

NAKED BEFORE THE FATHER

Published under the auspices of the

CENTER FOR MEDIEVAL AND RENAISSANCE STUDIES

University of California, Los Angeles

Humana Civilitas

*Studies and Sources relating to
the Middle Ages and the Renaissance*

Volume 9

EARLIER VOLUMES OF HUMANA CIVILITAS

1. *On Pre-Modern Technology and Science: Studies in Honor of Lynn White, jr.*, edited by Bert S. Hall and Delno C. West. 1976. 233 pages.
2. *The King's Progress to Jerusalem: Some Interpretations of David during the Reformation Period and Their Patristic and Medieval Background*, by Edward A. Gosselin. 1976. 131 pages.
3. *The Politics of an Erasmian Lawyer, Vasco de Quiroga*, by Ross Dealy. 1976. 33 pages.
4. *Persian Medical Manuscripts at the University of California, Los Angeles: A Descriptive Catalogue*, by Lutz Richter-Bernburg. 1978. xxii + 297 pages.
5. *Rhetoric and Poetic in Thomas More's "Utopia,"* by Arthur F. Kinney. 1979. 36 pages.
6. *Tenth-Century Latinity: Rather of Verona*, by Peter L. D. Reid. 1981. xiii + 158 pages.
7. *Ovid's "Metamorphoses": An Index to the 1632 Commentary of George Sandys*, by Christopher Grose. 1981. xiv + 154 pages.
8. *The Discourse of "Il Principe,"* by Michael McCanles. 1983. xxi + 142 pages.

Naked Before the Father
The Renunciation of Francis of Assisi

Richard C. Trexler

PETER LANG
New York · Bern · Frankfurt am Main · Paris

The emblem of the Center for Medieval and Renaissance Studies reproduces the imperial eagle of the gold *augustalis* struck after 1231 by Emperor Frederick II (Elvira and Vladimir Clain-Stefanelli, *The Beauty and Lore of Coins, Currency and Medals* [Croton-on-Hudson, 1974], fig. 130 and p. 106).

Library of Congress Cataloging-in-Publication Data

Trexler, Richard C.
  Naked before the father : the renunciation of Francis of Assisi / Richard C. Trexler.
   p. cm. — (Humana civilitas; vol. 9)
   Bibliography: p.
   Includes index.
   1. Francis, of Assisi, Saint, 1182-1226. 2. Asceticism—History—Middle Ages, 600-1500. 3. Christian saints—Italy—Assisi—Biography. 4. Assisi (Italy)—Biography. I. Title. II. Series: Humana civilitas; v. 9.
BX4700.F6T67 1989
271'.3'024—dc 19
[B]
ISBN 0-8204-0931-6
ISSN 0742-115 X

88-38475
CIP

CIP-Titelaufnahme der Deutschen Bibliothek

Trexler, Richard C.:
Naked before the father : the renunciation of Francis of Assisi / Richard C. Trexler. — New York; Bern; Frankfurt am Main; Paris: Lang, 1989.
 (Humana Civilitas; Vol. 9)
 ISBN 0-8204-0931-6

NE: GT

© Peter Lang Publishing, Inc., New York 1989

All rights reserved. Reprint or reproduction, even partially, in all forms such as microfilm, xerography, microfiche, microcard, offset strictly prohibited.

Printed by Weihert-Druck GmbH, Darmstadt, West Germany

For Sabrina and Christy

CONTENTS

Acknowledgments	ix
List of Illustrations	xi
Abbreviations	xiii

Introduction — 1

1. The Real and the Holy Family of Francis of Assisi — 7
    The Documents 7
    The Family Tree 11
        Genealogical Table 14
    The Family Properties 21

2. The Renunciation of Francis According to the Word — 31
    Boy Francis 31
    Francis at Twenty-Five 36
    The Francis of Bonaventure 40
    Renunciations 42
        Exchanging Money 43
        Tainted Money 48
        The Guilt of Francis 52
    Mother Pica Revealed 59

3. The Renunciation According to the Pictures — 71
    Four Duecento Renunciations 74
    The Renunciation in the Fourteenth Century 88
    The Renunciation in the Renaissance 97

4. Conclusion   103

Appendix. The Renunciation in the Primary Lives of
         Francis of Assisi   111
   1 Celano   111
   Julian of Speyer   112
   The Three Companions   113
   2 Celano   114
   Bonaventure, Legenda maior   114

Bibliography   117
Index   127
Illustrations

Acknowledgments

This book began as a lecture at the Walters Art Gallery, Baltimore. It inaugurated the exhibit God's Minstrel: St. Francis of Assisi (6 March–25 April 1982), celebrating the eight-hundredth anniversary of the birth of Francis. By then, years had passed since I had studied medieval history proper, indeed a score since, as a student at Frankfurt am Main, I had explored the subject of Francis-paintings with Harald Keller. So there was no obvious reason for the Walters to ask me to address its guests. I want to thank the organizer of the exhibit, Vicki Porter, for her confidence.

Many friends and scholars read parts of the manuscript, or made suggestions, or responded to my queries, and I am grateful to them all. They include Roberto Abbondanza, Elizabeth A. Beatson, Ignatius Brady, the late Edith Cooper, Sharon A. Farmer, Rab Hatfield, Carol D. Lanham, Donald Preziosi, Randolph Starn, the late James Stubblebine, Bernice J. Trexler, and Daniel Williman. I especially want to thank Dieter Blume and Christiane Klapisch-Zuber for their extensive criticism and encouragement. Generously, William Cook and Rona Goffen let me read typescript materials on Francis. The Franciscan Institute at St. Bonaventure University and the Vatican Library went out of their way to facilitate my research.

Finally, by giving me its Art Council chair for two academic quarters, the Department of Art, Design, and Art History at the University of California at Los Angeles afforded me the time and ambience in which to revise this work for publication. I am grateful as well to the University Center at Binghamton, State University of New York, for release time.

List of Illustrations

Unless otherwise indicated, the title of each work is "The Renunciation of St. Francis of Assisi." All known Renunciations are inventoried in this list. These illustrations appear together in a separate section after p. 129.

1. Master of the Bardi St. Francis, Florence
2. Follower of Guido da Siena, Siena
3. Master of St. Francis, Assisi
4. Anonymous, Gubbio
5. Anonymous, detail, Gubbio
6. Anonymous, Gubbio
7. Assisi Master, Assisi
8. Giotto di Bordone, Florence
9. Anonymous, Kloster Königsfelden
10. Paolo da Venezia, Venice
11. Anonymous, San Ginesio (Marches)
12. Anonymous, Todi
13. Anonymous, Verona
14. Master of the Franciscan Temperas, Ottana (Sardinia)
15. Taddeo Gaddi, Florence
16. Taddeo Gaddi, "Arbor Vitae," Florence
17. Anonymous, "The Crucifix of San Damiano Talking to Francis of Assisi," Assisi
18. Anonymous, "Pietro di Bernardone Beating Francis of Assisi," Assisi
19. Anonymous, Florence
20. Sassetta, London
21. Benozzo Gozzoli, Montefalco
22. Francesco Squarcione, Padua
23. Anonymous, Rome
24. Anonymous, "Pietro di Bernardone Beating Francis of Assisi," Baltimore
25. Anonymous, Baltimore

26. Domenico Ghirlandaio, Florence
27. Franciabigio, "The Marriage of Mary and Joseph," Florence
28. Anonymous (Nuremberg, 1512)
29. Jan Provost or Jan Gossart, England (?)
30. Li T'ien-to, lost since 1982
31. Ernest Wante, "Stultitia Crucis," Antwerp
32. Cartoon, Marvel Comic Book

Abbreviations

AF	*Analecta Franciscana*, vol. 10 (unless otherwise indicated)
JS	Julian of Speyer, *Vita Sancti Francisci*
LM	Bonaventure of Bagnoregio, *Legenda maior*
LMin	Bonaventure of Bagnoregio, *Legenda minor*
TS	*Legenda trium sociorum*, ed. T. Desbonnets
1 Celano	*Vita prima sancti Francisci*
2 Celano	*Vita secunda sancti Francisci*

Introduction

When his father [Pietro] saw [Francis] living so villainously, he was filled with great sorrow. Because he used to get enjoyment from [his son], he was ashamed. And he complained about him so much that, seeing his flesh almost dead from severe affliction and cold, he cursed him every time he saw him.

Since [Francis] was exposed to his father's maledictions, the man of God got a certain poor and despised little man [to defend him] against his father, and said to him: "Come with me and I'll give you some of the alms that are given to me. But when you see my father cursing me, I will then say to you: 'Bless me, father.' You [will then] take my father's place and make the sign of the cross over me and bless me." When then this poor man blessed him [while his father cursed him], the man of God said to his father: "Don't you know that God can give me a father who will bless me against your curses?"[1]

The story of Francis of Assisi is common coin of the European inheritance. An Italian merchant's son, wanting to be a knight, becomes instead the vassal of Jesus Christ. Breaking with his father and becoming a beggar, the boy emerges as the founder of a great religious order and a

---

1. My translation. The Latin is from T. Desbonnets, ed., "*Legenda trium sociorum*, Edition Critique" (abbreviation: *TS*), *Archivum Franciscanum Historicum* 67 (1974) ch. VII, 23. The edition begins at p. 89. The quotation is repeated in ch. I, 7 of Tommaso da Celano's second Life of Francis (2 Celano): *Legenda S. Francisci Assisiensis*, in *Analecta Franciscana* 10 (*AF*) (Quaracchi 1926–1941), the edition beginning on p. 131. Along with *TS* and 2 Celano, the following texts are referred to often in what follows. 1 Celano: in *AF*, pp. 10ff; Julian of Speyer (*JS*): in *AF*, pp. 335ff; Bonaventure of Bagnoregio, *Legenda maior*, (*LM*): in *Opera omnia* 8 (Quaracchi 1898) 504ff. The limited data in Bonaventure's *Legenda minor* (*LMin*), and Jacopo da Voragine's few unoriginal lines on the renunciation, are, respectively, in *Opera omnia* 8. 565ff and *AF*, p. 682. I will refer to other early Lives as occasion demands. The sections of the five main *vite* that deal with the renunciation are in the Appendix.

defender of the poor. Francis controls his own fate: his father does not disinherit him, but rather, the saint, after a fashion, disinherits the father. Francis does live out his life in obedience to all authority. Yet he deeply affects those in power, as well as others, by his purity of purpose and action. So natural was he that he talked to the animals, so selfless that it was said he took on Jesus' stigmata from the nails of the Cross.

The simplicity of the story is its genius. Its mythic base—the polarities between rich and poor, young and old—affords a plasticity that allows each passing age to imagine Francis as its own. No reader or viewer of the biographies of Francis of Assisi can fail to be impressed by the way different ages have shaped his story to serve their needs. Just among modern and contemporary images, we easily see how notions of Francis have changed to fit the altered styles and contexts of our lives (figs. 31 and 32).

Students of secular or sacred heroes will not be surprised. In every epoch, this story of the youth who renounced wealth for poverty needs recasting so as to edify ages that march to different drummers. Modern scholarship on Francis may sound different from the traditional kind, when it claims to uncover what *really* happened by bravely "stripping away" illusions, but often, modern scholars still mean to edify us.[2] This is understandable if regrettable. The life of Francis is impressive on its face.

Among the many tales in the Francis story, that of the saint's relations with his kin family has always been particularly susceptible to manipulation by different ages. Just as the cultural essence of the myth is that Francis achieved immortality by renouncing marriage and children and thus material possessions, so its social essence is that Francis the individual renounced his kin family to form the Franciscan family. Because every age shapes and defines its notions of natural and artificial kin families differently, every age has needed to retell the story. This book is about the event, and its retellings.

In the retellings, the needs of the times have occasionally seemed more important than the requirements of accuracy. As we shall see, Francis's own

---

2. A bibliographical overview is offered by M. Habig, ed., *St. Francis of Assisi: Writings and Early Biographies* (Chicago 1973) 1671-1760. See the three volumes issued on the eighth centenary: *S. Francesco d'Assisi. Documenti e archivi; Chiese e conventi; Storia e arte* (Florence: Electra, 1982). The film *Brother Sun, Sister Moon* by Franco Zeffirelli is a recent example of secular edification, as is the comic book *Francis, Brother of the Universe* (New York: Marvel Comics, 1980); see one of its cartoons, in fig. 32, below. L. White, jr., converted Francis into the saint of ecologists: *Machina Ex Deo: Essays in the Dynamism of Western Culture* (Cambridge, Mass. 1968) 91-94. The best recent biography of Francis is R. Manselli, *San Francesco d'Assisi* (Rome 1980), though it lacks a scholarly apparatus.

assumed kin family in that small but strategic hill town of Assisi, lying between Spoleto and Perugia,[3] died out quickly, so they contributed little to our knowledge of the family. The duty of telling the story was rather taken up by the Franciscan order, and for centuries, Franciscans have had their own, often conflicting agendas in describing Francis's early life. If it served their interests or those of their lay supporters, Francis's father Pietro di Bernardone and his mother, later named as Pica, might be made to stem from Italian stock or foreign, to be of noble or bourgeois backgrounds, of good character or bad, as long as Francis and his parents were represented as "decent." Modern secular scholars have themselves not been averse to edifying contemporary readers by reshaping Francis and his elders.

In truth, Franciscans and modern secular historians have been more interested in Francis's spiritual descendants—the generals, preachers, scholars, and missionaries of the Franciscan order: except when Francis's carnal family could be made over into a type of the Holy Family of Joseph, Mary, and Jesus, it was less interesting. Indeed, Franciscans claimed early on that their spiritual father had been born more like Christ than like the other children of Assisi—born almost of the spirit to a Virgin Mary-like mother. Similarly, modern secular historians have been more concerned with the symbol Francis became than with his carnal ancestry, which they usually define as having been typically middle class.[4]

My own study of Francis has, however, convinced me that his natural family was exceptional and relevant to his later life. In my view, the continuing requirements of the Franciscan order and of the Christian possessing classes have helped to obscure our knowledge and understanding of Francis's carnal family. Legend has been piled on legend, myth on myth, to the point that the most cautious historians, operating with treacherous sources, can find themselves assuming to be true things that are not well documented. But there is no gainsaying an attempt to clarify the matter. The first

---

3. A papal description of Assisi from 1288: "Assisi civitas brevi concluditur spatio": A. Toaff, *The Jews in Medieval Assisi 1305-1487* (Florence 1979) 4. That is about all that is known of the vital statistics of Assisi in this age. See further A. Fortini, *Assisi nel Medio Evo* (Rome 1940).

4. The best work on the family of Francis is L. Bracaloni, "Casa, casato e stemma di S. Francesco," *Collectanea Franciscana*, 2 (1932) 520-534; 3 (1933) 81-101. See also A. Fortini, *Nova vita di S. Francesco* (4 vols. Assisi 1959), 2.21-129. A main source for Francis as Christ is Bartholomeus de Pisa, *De conformitate vitae beati Francisci ad vitam domini Jesu* (2 vols. Quaracchi 1906-1912) (=AF, vols. 4-5). Also H. W. van Os, "St. Francis of Assisi as a second Christ in Early Italian painting," *Simiolus* 7 (1974) 115-132. The way hagiographers handled the families of saints in general is considered by D. Weinstein and R. Bell, *Saints and Society* (Chicago 1982).

purpose of this work is to study the history of the kin of Francis of Assisi, and establish the best possible family genealogy.

If Francis's elders were all this work was about, only the antiquarian could be expected to read further. After all, the real history beneath a cultural myth hardly matters in itself. But there is more here than the genealogy of Francis. Once we know what Francis's carnal family was actually like, we can understand better what his myth means and why the legend of Francis has proved so tenacious. As the story of Anastasia shows, our present age still constructs non-kin solidarities around reshaped stories, and describes them through words and pictures. The process of reconstructing Francis's real family can help us understand how that process of fictionalization works.

It is precisely the famous story of Francis's renunciation of worldly goods, an act done around 1206 when the future saint was some twenty-five years old, that proves central in unraveling the social and cultural meanings of Francis's story. The tale of how Francis left material life behind by dramatically removing his clothes in front of his father and the local bishop—soon after to put on celibate clerical eternity—is one Christian formulation of the concept of transgenerational continuity, that cultural continuity depends upon relations between men and not upon biology.[5]

Thus a second purpose of this work is to study Francis's renunciation as the story was variously told in the early centuries, so as to grasp how these different narrators imagined Francis to fit into, or to inform, such cultural continuities. Once the most probable history of Francis's kin family has been reconstructed, therefore, I shall ask what and who it was that Francis actually renounced, as compared to what and whom his older biographers said he renounced.

These are matters of fact, to be sure, but such facts are of limited importance until they are placed in contexts. If Francis renounced familial property, one must know if it was his mother's or father's property that was in question. But the social and conceptual context must be understood as well. We must ask about society's view of the *gender of wealth*. If however

---

5. The notion has been fruitfully studied by N. Munn, *Walbiri Iconography* (Ithaca 1973). See more recently the work of M. Godelier, *La production des grands hommes* (Paris 1982). Previously on the renunciation and surrounding events, see M. De Beer, *La conversion de saint François selon son premier biographe Thomas de Celano* (Paris 1963). The work has limited scientific value. A review article on De Beer's book, despite its title, does not examine the renunciation: G. Miccoli, "La 'conversione' di san Francesco secondo Tommaso da Celano," *Studi medievali*, 3rd ser. 5 (1964) 775–792. The confusion of words is explained by events: Francis renounced his inheritance about 1206. While he lived poor thereafter, he did not assume religious garb until about two years later. Scholars can differ as to when he "converted," and when he "left the world."

Francis renounced not so much property as dependence on his carnal family, we must comprehend what it meant at the time to be *dependent*—and independent. Notions of dependence, gender, and generations have changed over time, and have informed successive retellings of the Francis story.

People make images of past events, and in the case of Francis's renunciation, we are fortunate to have three distinct types of images from the first three centuries after his death. Perhaps the oldest is the Latin written tradition, formulated during the middle third of the thirteenth century by and for the male clergy. This clerical image of the renunciation is not without its problems, however. The thirteenth century is an age in which data on lay social conditions and mentalities are difficult to obtain, and indeed, scholarly monographs on Umbria's lay institutions are relatively scarce. Thus it will remain hard to compare to other records what the Latin writers say about Italian society of the time.

For all that, these Latin *vite* are invaluable. They begin with the first Life by the friar-priest Tommaso da Celano, written in 1228, the year of Francis's canonization, just two years after the holy man's death in 1226. Friar Julian of Speyer wrote the next Life of Francis, between 1232 and 1235. The third account is that of the so-called Three Companions, finished by 1246. Tommaso da Celano weighed in with his second *vita* in 1247–1248. Finally came the authoritative *Legenda maior* by the Franciscan minister general Bonaventure of Bagnoregio, written in 1263.[6]

The second image-type of the renunciation comprises the paintings of the story, almost all of them done between the second third of the thirteenth century, when the Latin Lives were written, and the later fifteenth century. They are no less important; indeed, they may be more crucial than the written texts for anyone interested in how the story was understood by the general public. For, generally speaking, the pictures of Francis were meant to edify not just the religious community, but large lay audiences, perhaps especially illiterates, who were thought more capable of grasping the flesh than the Word, as clerks were wont to say.[7]

Some pictures of the renunciation were painted in Umbria, of course.

---

6. See the bibliographical references in note 1, and more biographical information on the authors further below. In earlier times the authenticity, derivation, dates, and chronological order of certain of these sources were vividly contested: J. R. H. Moorman, *The Sources for the Life of St. Francis of Assisi* (Manchester 1940). My datings and characterizations here and in what follows reflect what seems to be a modern consensus. See the consensus as described by Fausta Casolini in Celano's *Vita di S. Francesco d'Assisi e Trattato dei Miracoli* (Assisi 1982), pp. xxxiii–xxxvii, with bibliography.

7. A near contemporary, the Parisian Peter the Chanter, grappled with the problem of the class character of images: R. Trexler, *The Christian at Prayer: An Illustrated Prayer Manual Attributed to Peter the Chanter (d. 1197)* (Binghamton 1987).

But the theme was perhaps even more popular in Tuscany. The concentration of surviving paintings of the renunciation in Tuscany is particularly welcome for a student wishing to grasp contemporaries' notions of Francis's social milieu. For Tuscany, unlike Umbria, is rich in primary sources and scholarly studies of the age covered by these paintings. These paintings can be placed in a Tuscan social context.

Since the pictures at our disposal range over a longer period than the Latin written sources, they will allow us to investigate not just what happened, but how the paintings of Francis's renunciation addressed changing concerns about the young, about gender, about dependence, and about property. Here we can profit from the interaction over time of written and painted sources—to grasp, for instance, how fifteenth-century paintings used texts of the thirteenth century, and especially the authoritative 1263 text of Bonaventure.

The last image that illuminates the facts about and meaning of the renunciation is again a written one, but this time in the Italian language rather than Latin. Part of the actual history of the renunciation has been preserved in certain hitherto overlooked Italian texts. This vernacular history of the renunciation may come from popular rather than clerical sources: it fits the social experience of contemporary lay audiences *and* the evidence of the pictures better than the Latin Lives do. In this part of the work, I show that there were different clerical and vernacular tracks for talking about generations, genders, and dependencies.

I do not mean to offer a general assessment of Francis's life. My study aims only at better delineating Francis in his passage from boyhood to manhood and from secular to religious preoccupations. It shows also how the story of that passage has served the agendas of early writers, artists, and audiences. With a better understanding of Francis's renunciation, a more judicious assessment of his later life may be possible. But such an assessment lies beyond the intention of this work.

1

The Real and the Holy Family of Francis of Assisi

THE DOCUMENTS

We cannot know who and what it was that Francis renounced in the *saeculum* without reconstructing his earthly family. So that is where to begin. Specialists have long maintained that certain family members, if not Francis himself, are found in a group of notarized documents that begin in 1215 and end in the year 1347, when the family disappears. These specialists may be wrong; the notarial family could be unrelated to Francis. For reasons I shall presently outline, however, I believe it is. I share the assessment that the most important genealogical data about Francis's family come from these documents.[8]

But most scholars rely only on the information in the written Lives or *vite*, especially because it is these sources and not the notarial documents that contain the most information about Francis's immediate family. These

---

8. It cannot be proved that the notarial family is indeed Francis's by finding in the notarial documents names mentioned in the *vite*. Only one relative—Francis's father—is named in the *vite*, and he is not named in the notarial documents; see below. That assessment rests rather on a preponderance of the evidence, which will be reviewed in what follows. The last certain date when descendants are mentioned in these notarial documents is 1347, when fra Francesco di fu Ciccolo di Piccardo and his sister, the nun Francesca, received a legacy. See however a Ciccolo, proctor of S. Francesco, apparently active in 1352: C. Cenci, ed., *Documentazione di vita assisana, 1300–1530*, 1 (Grottaferrata 1974) 99–100, 109. G. Zaccaria, "Diario storico della basilica e sacro convento di S. Francesco in Assisi (1220–1927)," *Miscellanea Francescana* 63 (1963) 90–120; see the continuation on the Trecento, ibid. 290–361. A document assigned to 1381 says that "ulterius non processit genealogia S. Francisci, deficiens in mortalitate," that is, by plague: L. Bracaloni, *La chiesa nuova di S. Francesco converso, casa paterna del Santo in Assisi* (Todi 1943) 5. Comparing the names in this genealogy to the notarial records of the members of the family listed in it shows that the genealogy contains obvious errors; for these records, see Cenci, *Documentazione*.

Lives name as Francis's father Pietro di Bernardone. They characterize his mother by reputation; her apparent name—Pica—is given in only one Life, that of the Three Companions, and there only in a derivative part of the manuscript tradition.⁹ Just two sources say that Francis had a "carnal" brother, otherwise unnamed, who mocked Francis for choosing poverty. Historians have interpreted "carnal" to mean a full flesh brother, as distinct from one of the spirit. They have not recognized that "carnal brother" always means a "uterine brother" but does not necessarily point to a common father.¹⁰

Other information about the immediate family in the Lives is scarce indeed. One source hints at a larger family unit: the Three Companions say

---

9. Pica's name is not found in Desbonnets' critical edition: *TC*. Nor is it in the *Legenda trium sociorum* edited by M. Faloci Pulignani, in the *Miscellanea francescana di storia, di lettere, di arti* 7 (1898) 81ff. In the literary sources, Pica's proper name first surfaces in early fourteenth-century sources like the Sarnano manuscript of *TS*; see Habig, *St. Francis*, p. 890. The scribes may have discovered it in the notarial documents, so the notarial family cannot be assumed to be Francis's merely because Pica is found there; see this error in Bracaloni, "Casa" 525. The link between the saint and the notarial family headed by Pica does, however, become if not certain, at least probable, through a series of prose genealogies all dated in and about 1381, which generally mirror the notarial documents: text in Bracaloni, "Casa" 85. Why the mother's name was probably not Giovanna, as indicated in one secondary legend, is explained below, note 49. Note that Pietro, who in the Lives is indubitably *filius Bernardonis*, is referred to there by the variant formula "Petrus de Bernardone" (1 Cel, *JS*) as well as with the standard formula "Petrus Bernardonis" (*TS*, 2 Cel, *LM*). Similarly, the usual genitive "Piche" referring to the mother in the notarial documents is once varied by "de Pica"; see the texts further below. These variants do, therefore, indicate parentage, and are not locative or family names. In her edition of Celano's *Vita* (p. 60), Casolini explains that the usage "de Bernardone," etc., is "la forma volgare umbra" for reference to a parent.

10. Celano and Bonaventure never refer to Pica as *mater carnalis*. They commonly refer to Pietro as *pater* and also as *pater carnalis*, with the latter seemingly meant to distinguish Pietro from the heavenly father, e.g., 2 Celano I, 7; *LM*, II, 4. But the most reliable source on the renunciation, the Three Companions, *never* calls Pietro *pater carnalis*, while on the one occasion they and 2 Celano refer to the brother, he is *frater eius carnalis*: *TS*, I, 2; III, 9; VI, 16-20; VII, 23; 2 Celano I, 7. So is he in Voragine: *AF*, p. 682. The 1381 genealogy mentioned in note 8 contains the first naming of Angelo as Francis's brother.

Donato Velluti (*La cronica domestica di messer D.V., scritta fra il 1367 e il 1370, con le addizioni di Paolo Velluti, scritte fra il 1555 e il 1560*, ed. I. Del Lungo and G. Volpi [Florence 1914]), shows that just as perforce "carnal nephews" and "carnal cousins" are related through only one parent, so might a "carnal brother" or sister be. That is the only way the formulation "fratello carnale di padre e di madre" (ibid., 106, 137, 295) makes sense. The formulation "through the same and through varied mothers" ("fratelli e sorocchie carnali e di diverse madri" [ibid., 295]) shows that the mother was the necessary carnal parent. I wish to thank C. Klapisch-Zuber for discussing these Velluti references with me; my reading of them is my own. On the "carnal brother" as uterine, and for the suggestive designation *carnales germani*, indicating that only *germani*, or children through both parents, were fully related, see G. Du Cange, *Glossarium mediae et infimae latinitatis*, s.v. "carnalis."

that his mother loved Francis "more than any of her other children," implying that she, but not necessarily Pietro, had at least three children.[11] However, Arnaldo Fortini thinks that the substantial notarial sources would have mentioned any other children, at least male ones, if Pica had indeed had more than these two.[12]

Fortini's argument is particularly persuasive and revealing because the notarizations, to which I now turn, deal richly, and exclusively, with Pica and her descendants. Three crucial facts emerge from an exhaustive review of that documentation:

1. *None of these documents ever mentions Pietro di Bernardone.*
2. *All of the documents refer to Pica—presumably a woman—directly or indirectly.*[13]
3. *All ascending references to Pica are made through only one son, Angelo di Pica.*

Thus, just as scholars have rightly surmised that the Pica of the notarial documents is the mother of Francis—though Francis is never named in these documents and Pica is not named in the *vite* until Three Companion manuscripts of the fourteenth century—so they have also decided, reasonably, that the brother of Francis referred to by the hagiographers is the Angelo of the notarial documents. We equate the two in what follows. But nowhere is it even intimated that any brother lived with Francis. Still, we may assume for now that the legal household included Francis, his mother, his father, and this brother, named Angelo.

According to the literary sources, Pietro was away in France when Francis was born in Assisi. The sources indicate that the mother promptly named the boy Giovanni, and that would suggest that she had him baptized before her husband returned. In any case, the Three Companions (I, 7) and

---

11. "Mater autem quia eum prae ceteris filiis diligebat": *TS*, III, 9.

12. Fortini, *Nova vita*, 2.95. See also G. Abate, ed., "Legenda S. Francisci Assisiensis," *Miscellanea Francescana* 39 (1939) 251.

13. Elsewhere I have found one male Pica: in a Sienese testament of 1348 by one evocatively named "Picardinus Francischi *domini* Pice." He was from Fabriano, near Assisi, in the Marches: *Archivio di Stato, Siena, Diplomatico, Spedale di S. Maria della Scala*, July 27, 1348. Samuel Cohn brought this to my attention; the Sienese archive director, Sonia Fineschi, kindly verified the reading. But in part because Pico was a known male name well before Francis's time, I do not think our notarial Pica was a man. I surveyed the indexes of the *Fonti per la storia d'Italia*, and along with many male Picuses, the one Pica I found was a Roman "Martinus Pica": *Fonti* 48.366 (1277). In addition to the standard classical encyclopedias, see Paul the Deacon for Pico the son of Saturn: ibid., 81.269; 51.6. Picuses in documents of the mid-twelfth century are found ibid., vol. 34 (see index for several); 98, pt. 3, p. 289; 101.35. Piccarda, incidentally, was a recognized female name: Velluti, *Cronica* 40, 50.

Celano's second Life (I, 1) say that when Pietro arrived home, he changed the name Pica had given the infant to Francis. Since Pietro here acted like a father, there seems little reason to doubt that he and Pica were married and that Francis was their legitimate issue.

There is good reason, on the other hand, to doubt that Angelo sprang from the same union. Here is another crucial fact to add to the three earlier ones:

4. *Neither the literary nor the notarial tradition says that Francis's brother, presumably Angelo, was Pietro's son.*

They do not say that the two lived in the same house, nor that Angelo worked alongside Pietro in Pietro's cloth shop, as would Francis. There is no indication of Angelo's occupation.

Scarcely anything is known about Francis's grandparents, but again, the location and thrust of the scanty evidence is significant. What is known of Pica's past comes from the notarial records, but what is known of Pietro's father comes exclusively from the literary tradition. Celano's first life has Francis deprecate his grandfather Bernardone as having been *rusticum, mercenarium, et inutilem*, a characterization whose closest translation might be "a useless country worker."[14] In one variant of the Three Companions, however, Bernardone is the merchant, his son Pietro—perhaps—dedicated to the soil.[15]

In fact, it is certainly wiser to assume that Pietro was the merchant the best sources make him out to be. He was a man who traveled to distant parts in pursuing his trade. According to these same sources, his son followed his father into the merchant life. Francis's sale of cloth from Pietro's warehouse would precipitate the boy's renunciation. Finally, the same *vite* imply that Pietro had lateral relatives in Assisi at the time of that decisive event.[16]

Turning to Pica, we find no indication either in the *vite* or in the notarial documents that Francis's mother had ascendants or lateral relatives liv-

---

14. 1 Celano I, 19. Compare to Dante's *Paradiso*, XI, 85–90:
>   Indi sen va quel padre e quel maestro
>   con la sua donna, e con quella famiglia
>   che già legava l'umile capestro;
>   né gli gravò viltà di cor le ciglia,
>   per esser fi' di Pietro Bernardone,
>   né per parer dispetto a maraviglia.

15. To "lucris terrenis": Abate, "Legenda," p. 376. The reference probably merely indicates "earthly goods," however.

16. It was *timore parentum*, presumably of Pietro's as events revealed, that the priest refused to take the money: 1 Celano I, 4; *LM*, II, 1.

ing in Assisi (or elsewhere, for that matter). Her first name is not given in any of the original literary sources, as I have noted. But if "Pica"—a word which some have thought to derive from the region "Picardy"—is her correct name, she could have been born in that French region as easily as in Assisi. Or perhaps her name simply indicates that she was the daughter of a salesman who traveled in Picardy, and was called Pica because her father was in Picardy just as Francis is said to have been named for France because his father had been there. Francis is said to have sung songs in broken French. If not through eventual foreign trips with his father or through his exposure to French soldiers before his conversion, this claim might be explained by his having had a French-speaking mother.[17]

THE FAMILY TREE

The very paucity of these gleanings from the literary sources, when combined with the remarkable fact, previously noted by Gemma Fortini, that the extant notarial tradition never mentions Pietro di Bernardone,[18] makes the picture some historians have painted of the holy family of Assisi a monument to human imagination. By the end of the sixteenth century, the origins of Pica, to whom scribes had given the wifely title "donna" in the fourteenth century, were being fixed in the nobility of Provence. Brother Ubaldo d'Alençon had her very family identified—that of the Bourlemont—and for the seventeenth-century savant Frassin that meant that Pica was related through marriage to the Roman descendants of Pope Gregory the Great![19] Less than a century ago, a scholar of Paul Sabatier's stature found nothing to preclude Pica's alleged Bourlemont roots.[20] As for Francis's noble roots, Friar Ubaldo long ago cited the so-called Chronicle of Grançey to prove them. Francis ". . . loved nobles more than he did anyone else. So he asked Our Lord devoutly to clarify from which line he derived. An angel responded to him that he came from the wife of a Roman senator."[21]

---

17. 1 Celano I, 7. The story itself may be a fiction, of course: French would have been the normal language for a "decent" songster wanting to act the knight. Definitely fictive is the ancient saw that the name Francis was first borne by our hero. For previous and contemporary Francises, see G. Abate, "Storia e leggenda intorno alla nascita di S. Francesco d'Assisi," *Miscellanea Francescana* 49 (1949) 368-369; M. Bihl, "De nomine S. Francisci," *Archivum Franciscanum Historicum* 19 (1919) 469-529, and especially 507 for the habit of naming infants after the land where the father traded.
18. G. Fortini, *Francesco d'Assisi ebreo?* (Assisi 1978) 22.
19. Bracaloni, "Casa" 83-84.
20. Ibid. 84, citing Sabatier.
21. Ibid. 84.

Nor did Pietro suffer genealogical neglect. Already by 1495 a Milanese incunable refers to the aristocrat *"messer* Pietro, one of the most noble persons of the city of Assisi, and one of the richest merchants of *Tuscany."* His family was that of the Moriconi, it was said.[22] The Tuscan commune to which that family belonged might be Pisa, Pistoia, or, in a work of 1895, even Florence; but Lucca was preferred from early on. Of course, Pietro too was linked to the ancients, notably to the emperor Justinian.[23]

Finally, even in the twentieth century there have been claims that the family of Francis on the mother's side was still alive.[24] By now, however, my point is made. By such "acrobatic" genealogies, inspired by nationalistic, regional, and—need it be said?—economic motives, both parents were made into "honorable" descendants of families with proper names, and fitted out with descendants who might stretch to the present.[25]

It is true that traces of such motivations still exist: how else explain the tenacious habit of assigning to Francis a family name—Bernardone—when this humble boy had none, or, as will be documented below, calling Pica in English "Lady Pica" when she was not noble? Still, generally speaking, modern historical writing has removed from its agenda the task of edifying regions and families. This is shown by Gemma Fortini's recent speculation that Pietro actually came from a Jewish family, an idea that only a few years ago would have been taken by many as an insult to the saint's memory.[26] But modern scholarship has not set aside all such ideological presumptions. As another instance, historians have never doubted that Pietro and Pica married only once. They have never questioned the assumption that Francis renounced only his father and the father's things. No one has doubted that Francis grew up in, and then renounced, what historians have called the *casa paterna*.

Given the patriarchal and patrilineal nature of Western societies, there is little mystery in the fact that no clerical or lay writer has ever entertained doubts on this score. But the reasons why early modern European historians searched out Francis's blood ancestry, and emphasized it so much, do bear review. First, not just the parents, but also a saint's lateral and descendant relatives participated in his or her aura, so such persons did everything they could to foster the saint's reputation. Indeed, these relatives were often

---

22. Ibid. 88.
23. Ibid. 89.
24. Ibid. 87.
25. Bracaloni, "Casa," pp. 83-93, traces and demolishes these "acrobatic" genealogies up through and including those in Fortini's *Nova vita*, 2, pp. 293-300.
26. G. Fortini, *Francesco d'Assisi ebreo?*

the key figures in creating and maintaining a cult.[27] Though the fanciful genealogies of past historians may bemuse us today, we should recognize that preserving and ennobling the ascendancy and descendancy of a remarkable man or woman was *and is* often one fundamental part of *making* a saint: many heroes of the past are unknown today because their relatives did not tend to their honor.

Second, the "father of a saint" and "the mother of a saint" were themselves considered somewhat cunning or mysterious persons, whose status was of relevance to the whole community. Indeed, the law makers of Italian communes sometimes voted them special privileges. Thus medieval societies began to maintain the honor of their fledgling saints by claiming that they came at least from "decent, if not noble" parents. So ingrained is that communitarian notion that even today, some scholars writing in English declare, with no foundation whatever, that contemporary documents always referred to Francis's mother as Lady Pica.[28] Such impulses are comprehensible. So-called "archaic" understandings of how the spirit of extraordinary men and women is generated from matter, so naively stated in thirteenth-century sources, are not foreign to our contemporary mentality. We still prefer holy, "better," families for our saints.[29]

That having been said, it is time to study Francis's blessed hearth as would some devil's advocate. Let us begin with Piccardo di Angelo di Pica, a nephew of Francis who I will show worked to stimulate Francis's cult, and then move backwards in time from him. From Piccardo's generation we will return to his father Angelo, and finally to mother Pica. The results of the reconstruction I now undertake are summarized in table 1.[30]

---

27. The cycle of development from early times seems to have been: first the body of the incipient saint was owned by kin who profited from it. Then the community attacked the family that put it in danger it by using a familial cult to increase its own power. Finally the strong community honored its individual saints and their families. See P. Brown, *The Cult of the Saints* (Chicago 1981), esp. 24ff; also his *Society and the Holy in Late Antiquity* (Berkeley 1982), pt. 2; see also my *Public Life in Renaissance Florence* (New York 1980) 93. A case of a sixteenth-century Assisian receiving public aid because he was considered "de stirpe et vera cognatione divi Francisci de Assisio" is reported in Bracaloni, "Casa" 87.

28. A. Mockler, "Pietro Bernardone: An Unorthodox Character," in R. Gasnick, ed., *The Francis Book* (New York 1980) 29ff; the same error in Habig, *St. Francis*, p. 890. Bracaloni says that the title *domina* (which meant "wife" not "Lady") began in the fourteenth century; "Casa" 83.

29. The point seems to be to encourage average men and women to lead a "good Christian family life."

30. Based on a study of all the documents. Compare the results with those of A. Fortini, *Nova vita* 2.100.

14   CHAPTER 1

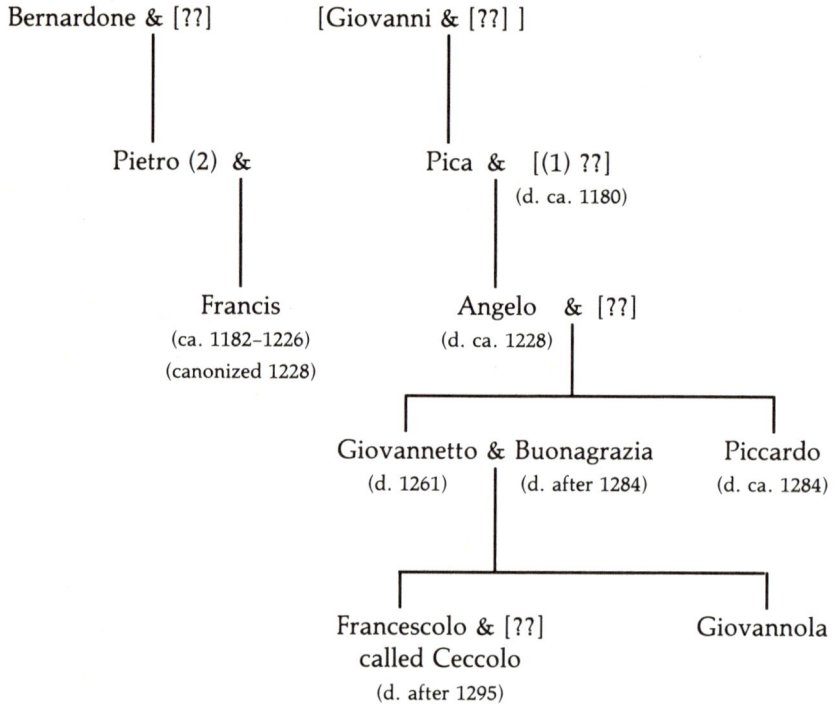

TABLE 1.
GENEALOGY OF FRANCIS OF ASSISI:
HYPOTHETICAL RECONSTRUCTION

We begin with Piccardo because he is so well documented, because he appears as a crucial link between two generations of Francis's relatives, and because he links in his person the sacred and profane worlds of Assisi. Piccardo di Angelo appears repeatedly in the notarial documents of the basilica of San Francesco because for twenty-eight years, from 1256 until 1284, he held the important position of *yconomus et procurator et syndicus* of that church and of its friars.[31] Since the individual friars were legally propertyless, Piccardo's office made him *the* legal person of the house in its relations

---

31. Zaccaria, "Diario" 90–112, esp. 93. Papal authorization to appoint a proctor at the basilica came only in 1240: ibid. 84. Piccardo is the third known person in this office: ibid. 84–85. In 1294–1295 Giovannetto's son Cecco or Ceccolo or Ciccolo (= Francesco), here mentioned for the last time, was the *syndicum procuratorem* not of the friars, but of the city council of Assisi, in its relations with the friars and their new syndic and proctor: ibid. 118–119. In

with the outside world, and the documents thus show him always acting as its agent. As syndic, Piccardo certainly had the right to go to law to recover legacies left to the friars or to their house. Piccardo imbursed and distributed the revenues given by the faithful for the use of the friary.

An early genealogy of Francis gives us further information about Piccardo. It says that he was a penitent, a *continens ordine penitentium sive continentium*. Even in mid-thirteenth century the outlines of this penitential grouping within the Franciscan family were becoming visible.[32] The order of penitents was composed mostly of elderly persons preparing to meet their maker. They took no solemn religious vows, but did have a place to assemble, a habit, and a rule. To enter the status of penitents, such persons might renounce ownership of goods. Penitents were "religious" or "pious persons" who, as far as their relations to the authorities were concerned, fell in the legal cracks between the laity and the clergy. Even in the later Middle Ages, the classification of penitents as "ecclesiastical persons" who fell personally and really either under episcopal or order jurisdiction, or as mere "pious persons" who along with their property might be under civil jurisdiction, depended on the power of each of these jurisdictions at any point in time.[33]

In our mid-thirteenth-century Assisian context, the Franciscan friars already were formally exempt from the jurisdiction of bishops. Piccardo and his property may thus have been exempt from the jurisdiction of the Umbrian commune, and subject only to superiors within the order. Francis himself had started as a penitent, and never became a priest. Assisian laymen who became penitents in this order that was making Assisi rich beyond its wildest dreams, almost certainly freed themselves, and their property, from

---

Florence, the civil office of the syndic minor was a vehicle through which the commune, acting as "neighbor" or "friend," ultimately controlled Franciscan income; see Trexler, "Death and Testament in the Episcopal Constitutions of Florence (1327)," now in my *Church and Community, 1200-1600. Studies in the History of Florence and New Spain* (Rome 1987) 268. "Syndics, proctors, actors, and *yconomi*" also resided semi-permanently in Rome as representatives of various orders, and Assisi at this time was "peculiarly productive" of such people: R. Brentano, *Two Churches: England and Italy in the Thirteenth Century* (Princeton 1968) 26, 32ff. J. Moorman, *A History of the Franciscan Order from its Origins to the Year 1517* (Oxford 1968) 120-121 has more on the early office in the order.

32. Fortini, *Nova vita* 2.96. On the penitents, see G. Casagrande, "Penitenti e Disciplinati a Perugia e loro rapporti con gli Ordini Mendicanti," in a special issue on *Les Ordres Mendiants et la Ville en Italie centrale (v. 1220-v. 1350)*, in *Mélanges de l'Ecole française de Rome. Moyen Age, Temps Modernes* 89 (1977) 711-721.

33. C. Piana, "La posizione giuridica del terz'ordine della penitenza a Firenze nel secolo XIV," *Archivum Franciscanum Historicum* 50 (1957) 49-73; Trexler, *Public Life* 34, with bibliography, esp. the reference to the treatise on the subject by Lapo da Castiglionchio.

civil intendance. That must have been especially true for the Franciscan proctor of Assisi. He wanted to adorn a church that in honoring his relative would enrich the city.

Arnaldo Fortini called Piccardo no less than the "chief animator" of the lower and upper church of Assisi.[34] No document describes him in this way, and the church itself already graced the local skyline when Piccardo assumed office. Yet the very continuity and duration of his position, first documented only three years after that church was definitively consecrated in 1253,[35] does support the inference that he was more than an ordinary officeholder. So does the office as it was sometimes tenured in those centuries. Laymen often became administrators of goods of a church as a condition of making an endowment to a religious body: thus they effectively remained in control of their own grants for as long as they lived.[36] Exempt from civil taxes, such persons thus assured their livelihoods by continuing to administer what remained their property in fact, even if it had become God's at law.

In my view, Piccardo not only had the desire to build a monument, but some money and important real property to do it with. To trace the source of this wealth, I begin with documents of 1253 and 1261, the former pinpointing Piccardo's own dowry for the church of his uncle, the latter illustrating the types of grants that testators—including one of Francis's nephews—were leaving for the fabric of the basilica. I proceed in reverse order.

Piccardo had a brother named Giovannetto di Angelo, who was the father of two children. On the occasion of an illness in 1261, Giovannetto dictated his last will and testament in Piccardo's house. Giovannetto left his estate to his children, but he named Piccardo in the latter's quality as proctor of San Francesco as his substitute heir in the event that the testator's son Francescolo as well as his daughter Giovannola should die before inheriting their father's estate. In case they died, Giovannetto said, their goods were to be applied "as Piccardo and the custodian of San Francesco thought best" for the particular goal Giovannetto had in mind: "for my soul and

---

34. Fortini, *Nova vita* 2.96.

35. Zaccaria, "Diario" 87, 90. The upper and lower churches had been under construction since the late 1220s, and the construction continued long after this date. See recently H. Belting, *Die Oberkirche von San Francesco in Assisi* (Berlin 1977); M. Boskovits, "Celebrazioni dell'VIII centenario della nascita di S. Francesco. Studi recenti sulla Basilica di Assisi," *Arte Cristiana*, n.s. 71 (1983) 203–214.

36. Religious institutions carefully weighed the value against the costs for estimated years of life then, as they do now; see my "Une table florentine d'espérance de vie," *Annales E.S.C.* 26 (1971) 137ff.

[those of] my antecedents, and for ill-gotten goods."[37] By identifying himself in the will as *Iohannectus olim Angeli de Pica*, he included among those antecedents his father and his paternal grandmother.

Giovannetto did not take the matter of ill-gotten goods (*male acceptis*) lightly. On August 5 of the same year he added a codicil to his testament that effectively gave the satisfaction for such usury precedence over his children's claims. Again in Piccardo's house, Giovannetto wrote: "I add with these codicils, that whether my children be alive or dead, I want my brother Piccardo to give and restitute from my goods, as he sees fit, [money] for the restitution of *male et illicite acceptorum vel pro usuris*, if I am found to have accepted [usury] at any time."[38]

At the risk of being summary, let us get to the heart of what was happening. First of all, in this age it was the bishop who determined whether a testator owed usury. Second, in a questionable procedure, bishops sometimes defined the children or relatives of the usurer as "poor," making use of the ancient Ambrosian dictum that charity begins at home. These kin could then imburse usured money, and thus defend patrimonies, in those cases where the usury was patent but its victim or victims unknown. Third, as "poor persons" by definition, Franciscan friars in the legal person of their proctor were also proper recipients of such generic debts or grants.[39] Jesus' dictum that to follow him, one should give what one had to "the poor," obviously had the most varied of applications.

In this framework, Giovannetto's actions make good sense. As procurator of San Francesco and as Giovannetto's brother, Piccardo was evidently the perfect defender of his nephew and niece, and of the friars, against those who might attempt to attach the estate in the court of the bishop.

37. "Pro anima mea et meorum antecessorum, et pro male acceptis, ad sensum Picardi et custodis S. Francisci"; Bracaloni, *Chiesa* 250.

38. "Addo . . . quod sive filii mei vivant sive moriantur, volo quod Picardus frater meus det et restituat de meis bonis ad suam voluntatem pro restauratione male et illicite acceptorum, vel pro usuris, si quas aliquando accepissem": ibid.

39. Perhaps significantly, on the eve of Piccardo's appearing as proctor, the friars had obtained papal authorization to receive just such sums *and* generic gifts: "ut de usuris rapinis et aliis male acquisitis, dummodo ii, quibus ipsorum restitutio fieri debet, nequeant inveniri; nec non de quibuslibet legatis indistincte in pios usus relictis . . . usque ad quingentas libras provisionorum recipere valeatis": Zaccaria, "Diario" 89 (1254). On the subject of episcopal authority and familial reimbursement, see my "Death and Testament" and "The Bishop's Portion: Generic Pious Legacies in the Late Middle Ages in Italy," both now in *Church and Community* 245–288, 289–356. On the definition of institutions as poor, see Trexler, "Honor and the Defense of Urban Elites in the Italian Communes," in F. Jaher, ed., *The Rich, the Well Born, and the Powerful* (Urbana 1973) 64–78.

Giovannetto's testament is representative of many testaments that named the friars, in the person of their proctor, as beneficiaries. Seeking to preserve their estates against creditors and against property-accumulating bishops, such testators recognized that the proctor of San Francesco was an ideal mediary. If he did his job right, usury with unidentifiable victims would pass through him to the friars. Since the latter were penniless and abstemious by law, monies unnecessary to their frugal sustenance could buy monuments in the basilica. In this and other such ways, wealth was actually recycled back into the economy, even while earning temporal and heavenly merit for the benefactors, who both clothed the needy and glorified God with monuments.[40]

For such testators did seek the salvation of their souls, and it was a bitter truism of the time that goods that ended up in the bishop's purse might bring perdition for everyone. The Franciscans grew rich precisely through such institutions and by the confidence and awe the friars inspired in the faithful. They consumed little, but through these institutions they produced glory and profit for their supporters.

The division-of-property document dated 1253 is just as important for the history of the saint's family as is Giovannetto's will of 1261 for Assisian ecclesiastical and economic history. In the 1253 text, Giovannetto assigns to Piccardo certain personal and real properties that the two had previously held in common. The direction of this transaction, from Giovannetto to Piccardo, offers the merest hint that Giovannetto may have been older than his brother: that possibility is substantially strengthened by the fact that Piccardo was still alive in 1284, twenty-three years after Giovannetto apparently died, leaving behind a widow and two children.[41] Second, since

40. Although the outlines of this process are clear, only a substantial study of available records of communal offices of the *syndicus procurator* or the syndic minor (Florence) will reveal how recirculation worked. The cases of Piccardo receiving testamental grants are the earliest I can find among the printed documentation: Zaccaria, "Diario" 90-91, 92, 96-97, 100-101, 102, 104 (Piccardo her fiduciary, she to be buried in the church), 105, 107 (payment by a judge to the custodian "pro restauratione malorum ablatorum et malorum consiliorum et negligentie et sententiarum iniuste datarum"), etc.

41. I assume Giovannetto's last appearance in the sources—in 1261—to be the year of his death. Piccardo was apparently seriously ill after 1278, but he is cited again in 1284: Zaccaria, "Diario" 105, 110ff. The 1253 document refers to "Piccardus et Iohannettus, filii quondam et heredes Angeli Pice, ad divisionem bonorum eorum hereditariorum mobilium et stabilium venientes": Bracaloni, *Chiesa* 248-249. The fact that this document is a Franciscan copy in the order's archive probably explains why Piccardo is listed first, in the precedential place due an elder: the order was keeping track of its official. Another reason to believe Giovannetto was older than Piccardo is *ad silentium*: "Iohannectus Angeli" twice appears as a witness in 1234; Piccardo never appears in Franciscan documentation until 1256, when he is proctor of S. Francesco: Fortini, *Nova vita* 2.96.

Piccardo appears as proctor for San Francesco in 1256, just three years after this division, it is plausible that the property he accepted in the division became a part of what we may call Piccardo's dowry for entering the order of penitents.

Was Piccardo motivated to agree to the property division in 1253 so as to obtain such a dowry? Or is the division at that date rather explained by Piccardo's having finally reached an age his father might have stipulated for division of the brothers' property? Such a stipulation was common testamentary procedure.[42] The former motivation proves to be more probable, but to demonstrate that, it must first be determined, in the absence of his testament, when father Angelo died and thus put his sons in joint ownership of his estate.

That happened sometime between 1215, when Angelo was still active, and 1228 or 1229 (Francis died in 1226 and was canonized in 1228). In a document of 1228 or 1229 (I shall label it "1228"), the authorities of Assisi assessed "the house of the sons of Angelo di Pica."[43] As has long been recognized, the wording of this assessment shows that Angelo had died. Now, who were these unnamed "sons of Angelo di Pica"? The answer is in the 1253 document. Since in that year Giovannetto and Piccardo divided inheritance, there is little doubt they were the ones who held the house in common in 1228. If any other son was alive in 1228, he had probably died by 1253.

Next, there is every reason to assume that grandmother Pica was dead by 1228, when Piccardo—presumably named after her—is known to have been among the living. For to follow the language of the age, Piccardo's parents in naming him "remade" the grandmother. Christiane Klapisch-Zuber has worked out the complex rules for this practice in Tuscany. It is true that the norms could have been slightly different in Umbria, where the practice has not been studied in such detail. But one rule was certainly as inflexible here among Italian Christians as it had been for ages among the Jews. With the rarest exceptions, renaming was done only after the death of the namesake. For close relatives like Angelo's mother, that meant as soon after death as possible.[44]

---

42. A typical example of such a testamental provision is reported in Trexler, "The Magi Enter Florence. The Ubriachi of Florence and Venice," now in my *Church and Community* 155 (thirty years of age).

43. "Filii Angeli Piche pro eorum domo dent et solvent VI lib. et mediam lucenses"; Bracaloni, *Chiesa* 247. *Angelus Pice* was twice witness to contracts in 1215: Fortini, *Nova vita* 3.589–590.

44. C. Klapisch-Zuber, "The Name 'Remade': The Transmission of Given Names in Florence in the Fourteenth and Fifteenth Centuries," now in her *Women, Family, and Ritual in Renaissance Italy* (Chicago 1985) 283–309. The system was in place in Assisi, Fortini noting

That suggests of course that Piccardo was newborn around 1228. This hypothesis would make him twenty-five years old when in 1253 the two brothers divided their common property, a reasonable minimum age that Angelo might have stipulated in his testament for division. But this hypothesis would also make him an improbably young twenty-eight years of age when in 1256 he is found as a penitent and the proctor of San Francesco. These statuses were commonly reserved for elders of forty-five years and up.

Basing an alternate hypothesis on this notion that "old age" set in at forty-five years of age would have Piccardo born around 1211; he would then have been forty-two years old when the brothers divided the property. But this is far beyond any plausible minimum age that Angelo would have stipulated for that division. Thus, the division of property probably did not take place when it did *because* the younger son had reached a minimum age.

The history of Giovannetto's family lends credence to this hypothesis. Giovannetto himself appears as a witness in 1234; if performing such a function required a majority of twenty-five years, he would have been born no later than 1208. A perhaps more substantial clue to Giovannetto's age comes from the fact that he baptized his only known son Francescolo. This suggests in the first place that Giovannetto's father, Angelo, was still alive at that point; otherwise, Giovannetto would have been called on to remake his father. Second and more significant, however, Giovannetto appears to have remade his uncle Francis, for the name was still not common at the time.

When then was Francescolo born? Since in his testament of 1261 Giovannetto made no tutorial provisions for him, Francescolo had certainly reached his majority of twenty-five years at that point; he was therefore born in 1236 at the latest. This was two years, we recall, after his father had served as a legal witness, a role often requiring marriage.[45] At the other extreme, the name Francis being otherwise uncommon, Francescolo was clearly born after Francis's death in 1226, probably shortly after the pompous canonization in Assisi in 1228. Like any father, Giovannetto would have rushed to remake such a saintly ancestor, so as to give his son all the civic honor that accrued to such relatives!

---

that names commonly recurred every other generation: *Nova vita* 2.9. But he did not mention that the "remade" person was almost always dead.

45. The available municipal statutes of Assisi were edited in 1469, but they sometimes have (undated) rubrics from as early as Francis's time: Fortini, *Nova vita* 3.206-207. The same author (*Assisi* 71) says that they "undoubtedly" reach back to the thirteenth century; one of the fourteenth century is noted below, at note 57. One printed statute requires sons to be twenty-five years old before they can make a contract without the assent of the mother or father: *Statuta*

If we assume that Francescolo was born in 1228, we can calculate plausible ages for his father, his grandfather, and his uncle Piccardo. Assuming that he was approximately twenty-five years of age when he married and when his son Francescolo was born, Giovannetto would have been born about 1203, and thus have been some fifty-eight years old at his presumed death in 1261. Angelo must have been born about 1178, dying at about fifty soon after Francescolo's birth. Piccardo certainly entered the world between 1204 and 1211. Finally, Pica: assuming that Pica was remade through Piccardo, these years between 1204 and 1211 indicate the approximate time of Pica's death. And since Pica was involved in the events that immediately preceded Francis's renunciation about 1206, the best estimate is that she died between 1206 and 1211. I will later suggest that her impending death might even have been precipitated by the renunciation.

THE FAMILY PROPERTIES

This laborious and speculative reconstruction of Piccardo's ancestors was justified by our need to know the proctor's age, but it was even more necessary in order to place in context our examination of one central question: the source of the properties that Giovannetto and Piccardo had inherited in 1228 and divided in 1253. Since both these documents name the boys' father, historians have reasonably assumed that the properties came from Angelo, who I have estimated died shortly after his brother Francis.

But where had Angelo gotten these properties, or any other part of his estate? The documents refer Angelo back to Pica. The name of Pietro, we repeat, does not occur in any notarial document. None the less, to this question of the source of Angelo's wealth, all previous scholars have answered: Angelo got his wealth from his father Pietro. Angelo, in short, was Pietro's natural heir.

---

magnifice civitatis Assisi (Perugia 1534–1543), bk. II, rub. 32 (cc. 10rv of the book). This makes Giovannetto's majority when he served as witness plausible; the document is in Fortini, *Nova vita* 2.98. Francescolo last appears in the records (as Ciccolo Ioannecti) in 1295: ibid. I do not agree with Fortini that he is identical with the later Ciccolo Iohangnoli (1316–1317), and I doubt the identification of Francescolo with Ciccolo *Piccardi* (1291–1332), given that they have different patronymics: ibid. Note that Cenci, *Documentazione* 1.45, 50, 54–55, 63ff, 73, 99, and 109, also avoids such identifications. If on the other hand this Ciccolo Piccardi is identical with Francescolo, my hypothesis that he was born about 1228 would make the latter ca. 100 years old at death. For the prehistory of the name Francesco, see the information above, at note 17, and for its subsequent use in the Tuscan countryside, see C. de La Roncière, "L'Influence des franciscains dans la campagne de Florence au XIVe siècle (1280–1360)," *Mélanges de l'École française de Rome. Moyen age. Temps modernes* 87 (1975) 27–103: it is rarely if ever given until 1280–1290; is wildly popular from then till ca. 1350; after which its use declines.

This appears to be wrong on at least four counts. First, neither the literary nor the notarial sources say that Pietro was Angelo's father. Second, the literary sources only identify a blood brother of Francis, and thus not one who is necessarily Pietro's son. Third, most of the available notarial documents, beginning in 1215, *and all those that deal with family property transactions in these crucial decades,* trace the genealogy of Angelo and his progeny to Pica, never to Pietro. The thesis that Angelo's properties, including the so-called *casa paterna* where Francis is supposed to have lived, had earlier been Pietro's, is questionable on a final count. Though allegedly wealthy merchants, Pietro's and his father Bernardone's very names, even in variant forms, do not appear in the genealogy of Pica until the fourth generation—a generation later, that is, than the name Francis.[46] All together, these facts seem decisive: the notion that Angelo's property was originally Pietro's is without foundation.

There are obstacles to the orthodox view at every turn. First, the very silence of the sources on Pietro, despite his unpleasant but prototypical opposition to his son's profession, is telling. For instance, I can find no hint of when Pietro died. If they could have, contemporaries in this strongly patrilineal society would have emphasized Piccardo's and Angelo's personal and propertied descent from Pietro rather than from Pica. How awkward, not to say demeaning, when describing property to refer to the mother but not to the father of a saint! If Angelo and his sons could have established a noble or honest patrilineage through Pietro di Bernardone, they would certainly have done so and not left the task for future generations of hagiographers.

This situation had an important implication for Pica's ancestry. The wish of her descendants to link themselves to their saintly relative, and especially Piccardo's professional need to do so, inhibited the whole line from elaborating on the ascendant or lateral relations of Pica. For any attention to them would draw attention away from Pica's descendants' link to Francis. Thus Pica remained the terminus of all contemporary genealogies of the descendants of Angelo, and the all-too-apparent source of their estate. She was the mother of a saint, and that was enough.

A second set of obstacles to the traditional view that Angelo's property came from his alleged father Pietro emerges from attempts to explain away the fact that Angelo is called the son of Pica rather than the son of Pietro.

---

46. On Pietruccio and Bernardo, see Fortini, *Nova vita* 2.100. It would have made sense for Cecco or Francesco, obviously named after the saint, to "remake" that saint's ancestors. The closest Fortini could come to an Angelo using part of his alleged father's name was one Angelo di Bernardone, cited in a document of 1213 unrelated to the family: ibid. 2.93, 100.

Least plausibly, it might be suggested that Pietro left his whole estate to his wife Pica, so that the inheritance of Angelo would naturally be derived through her in the notarial documents. Yet husbands normally only returned the wives' own property in wills. It would have been unusual indeed at the time for an Italian husband to pass his estate to his wife, and all the more so if, as we suspect, Pietro had relatives of his own.[47]

The argument that Angelo was called "of Pica" merely for convenience is more plausible. Take for instance "Angelo di Pica's" appearance as a third-party witness in 1215. It has been argued that this and similar ascendant references to the mother were used here as they were by other Assisians, because people recognized the person in question by referring to such an elder: in this particular instance, for example, it might be thought that Pica was referred to as the ascendant because she was alive but Pietro dead.[48] A closer look shows otherwise. In fact, it is not clear in what order Francis's parents died. Further, I have estimated that Pica died sometime between 1206 and 1211, well before the document of 1215.

But even if Pica died later, the traditional explanation for the use of her as the ascendant runs aground on the document of 1228. In it, Pica is given as the lineage source of "the sons of Angelo di Pica," although I have shown that she had to have been dead by then in order for Piccardo to remake her. This being so, in a transaction involving the inheritance of property, the notary would not have referred to the mother's ascendancy if Pietro had been Angelo's father or if he had been the past owner of the house that was taxed in that year.

There can be other reasons for using the mother's name in ascendance genealogy, and practices do indeed differ in different regions. But one must choose the most probable meaning of this practice, and the use of Pica's name as ultimate ascendant in the references to property in 1228, in 1253, and in 1261 would seem to make it almost certain that Angelo's possessions came from Pica. Along with the available genealogical information—which is far from complete but nonetheless consistent enough where it counts— it becomes altogether probable that Pietro had no blood relation to Angelo di Pica or to his descendants. What son would have failed to remake the

---

47. Typically, besides her depleted dowry, Giovannetto left his wife only "domus mee, donec honeste cum filiis meis ibi morari voluerit": Bracaloni, *Chiesa* 250. Studying Genoese wills of the time, S. Epstein did find an occasional husband who left his widow more than her dowry, but only one who stated categorically: "whether she remarries or not": *Wills and Wealth in Medieval Genoa, 1150-1250* (Cambridge, Mass. 1984) 109.

48. There is no substantial work on the use of matronymics in Umbria; see Fortini, *Nova vita* 3.589-590; 2.99. C. Klapisch-Zuber goes so far as to say that in Florence, a female given name never entered into ascendancies; "Name," in *Women* 285.

father of a saint on his death, or remake him again if such a namesake died? Thus, as Pietro recedes, the figure of mother Pica moves to the forefront of family importance. It may even be possible to recover something about her history from these stingy documents.

Common sense as well as the rules of remaking tell us that Angelo would have remade Pietro if in fact Pietro was his father. But Angelo named neither of the sons he orphaned in 1228 by that name. Rather, he named his second son Piccardo, almost certainly after his mother. He named his first son Giovannetto or little John—and this is the possible clue to Pica's life. It can be read in two ways. Perhaps the namesake of Giovannetto was Pica's father. This might explain the origins of the Three Companions' story that Pica herself had named Francis "Giovanni" before Pietro on returning from abroad changed the baby's name to Francis. In this reading, Pica would have tried unsuccessfully to remake her father, but Angelo succeeded in remaking his grandfather.[49]

Or perhaps Giovannetto's namesake was Angelo's long dead father and Pica's first husband. In this case the same Three Companions' story might preserve an echo of the marriage that produced Francis's older, assumedly uterine brother Angelo.[50] On reflection, however, this seems less likely than the previous hypothesis. For if Angelo had named his son Giovannetto after his father, he would have been more likely to call himself Angelo di Giovanni than Angelo di Pica.

It is however unnecessary to speculate beyond the generation of Pica. What is important is that Angelo left no children named after his alleged father, Pietro di Bernardone, and so his property surely did not come from Pietro. Following the same rule of thumb that ascendancy in name indicates property derivation, it must be assumed that rather than coming from his father, Angelo's property came from his mother. She is identified in property transactions as Angelo's ancestor because she owned the property when she passed it on to her son.

To summarize: just as Piccardo was named after his paternal grandmother, Giovannetto was most probably named after Pica's father. Angelo

49. The whole is in 2 Celano I, 1. Note that one legend says that Pietro's wife's name was Giovanna: A. Fierens, ed., "La question franciscaine: Le ms. II. 2326 de la bibliothèque royale de Belgique," *Revue d'histoire ecclésiastique* 8 (1907) 290. But the plausibility of both this unique statement, and that which says Francis was first named Giovanni, is suspect. Given the notion of Francis's "conformity" with Jesus, the link to St. John the Baptist is too convenient.

50. The faulty genealogy assigned to 1381 lists Angelo as *germanus* of Francis: cited in Bracaloni, "Casa" 85. But see above: Angelo may be no more than Francis's half-brother in the two literary primary sources where the "frater carnalis" is mentioned; this would necessarily make him older than Francis. See the reconstruction hypothesis above for a birth date about 1178, before Francis.

and his descendants were not related to Pietro. Instead, Pietro became Pica's second husband sometime around 1180, that is, shortly after Angelo's estimated birth in 1178. It remains uncertain whether the young Angelo continued to live with his mother or was given over to maternal relatives. In any case, from this new marriage of Pietro and Pica the sole known fruit was Angelo's half-brother, Francis of Assisi, who is estimated to have been born in 1182.

This genealogy has property implications. One target of our research is, of course, to identify the rights and properties Francis renounced. Therefore it is significant that while the notarial documents do not mention Pietro or that he owned anything, the same records do indicate that Pica was a propertied individual.

To overstate the matter slightly, one can suggest that the house in which Francis grew up was not a *casa paterna* but a *casa materna*. The family property that historians have most carefully followed is this so-called *casa paterna*, a location first identified in notarial documents as "the house of St. Francis" in 1398. For no persuasive reasons, some historians think that this house was part of Piccardo's property in the 1253 division with Giovannetto, or that it is implied as his in a document of 1281.[51] But what is significant is that Piccardo's property rights always refer back to Pica, and that the penitent Piccardo's association to that *casa* in 1253 is related to his position as proctor of the Franciscans.

Thus, even if Pietro was the rich merchant sketched by the Lives, the house in which he lived and the capital that financed his operations could have come from his wife. Pietro would not have been the first man to seem rich on his wife's property.[52] But let me be cautious, and say only that some of the things Francis renounced may have come from his mother.

What might have been the nature of such properties? An answer is difficult because we have no Assisian municipal statutes definitely of this date. But a perusal of the contemporary civil law tradition, aided by the work of the legal historian Manlio Bellomo, allows some initial generalizations. At first it might seem that as a typical widow about to remarry, Pica would have possessed only her dowry. It was becoming customary at the

---

51. Yet in the following year the house is said to have been owned by Piccardo's nephew and Francis's namesake Cecco, who "returns" it, to follow Bracaloni's words, to Piccardo: Bracaloni, *Chiesa* 248–253.

52. Marrying so as to use women's wealth was a time-honored means for young men to begin to build their own fortunes; see D. Owen Hughes, "From Brideprice to Dowry in Mediterranean Europe," *Journal of Family History* 3 (1978) 262–296; S. Chojnacki, "Dowries and Kinsmen in Early Renaissance Venice," *Journal of Interdisciplinary History* 5 (1975) 571–600; D. Herlihy and C. Klapisch-Zuber, *Les toscans et leurs familles* (Paris 1978); Klapisch-Zuber, *Women*.

time for a dowry to be considered a girl's one and only inheritance from her father: in effect the dowry increasingly amounted to a renunciation by the girl, an *exclusio propter dotem*, to any further claim on the paternal estate.[53] Pica's position may have been no better as regards her first husband. If he behaved as did most, his will would have cut off his surviving spouse from all but her dowry upon her remarriage to Pietro.

In the normal course of things, Pica would then have given the use of her dowry to her new husband Pietro, so the question is whether or not this dowry could have become a bone of contention between Francis and his father. It seems unlikely. Not only did Pietro have a right to dominion and control of the dowry for as long as Pica lived but also on her death the dowry would normally have passed either to a son "of the first bed" (Angelo), to a daughter, or back into the paternal family, but not to a son of a second marriage.[54] To be sure, there is no indication that Pica had living family, or a daughter. But for all that, it remains unpromising to hypothesize that Francis renounced a right to his mother's dowry.

Quite apart from Francis's renunciation, the genealogical ascendancy to her in all the property documents under review, in all but one case ("de Pica") through the genitive "Piche," does indicate that Pica had property other than her dowry. Whether willed to her by her father or her first husband—a practice not unknown, and indeed more common in the twelfth than in later centuries—such extradotal properties, similar to if later distinct from so-called paraphernalia at law, are more likely to have been a matter of contention between Francis and his father. This is for the simple reason that being Pica's husband would not have given Pietro any indisputable right to the control of such extradotal properties.[55]

53. For a later period, see T. Kuehn, "Some Ambiguities of Female Inheritance Ideology in the Renaissance," *Continuity and Change* 2 (1987) 11–36. In general: M. Bellomo, *La condizione giuridica della donna in Italia* (Turin 1970) 35–63.

54. On the normal players for the widow's dowry, see C. Klapisch-Zuber, "The 'Cruel Mother': Maternity, Widowhood, and Dowry in Florence in the Fourteenth and Fifteenth Centuries" and "The Griselda Complex: Dowry and Marriage Gifts in the Quattrocento," in *Women* 117–131, 213–246. On the preference for the first bed in the Justinian Code, see P. Fedele, "Vedovanza e seconde nozze," in *Il matrimonio nella società altomedievale*, 2 vols. (*Settimane di Studio del centro italiano di studi sull'alto medioevo*: Spoleto 1977) 828–829.

55. In the absence of Assisian statutes clearly identifiable as contemporary, I have relied on the study of Italian municipal statutes and jurisprudence by M. Bellomo, *Ricerche sui rapporti patrimoniali tra coniugi: Contributo alla storia della famiglia medievale* (Rome 1961). Note the emphasis of the fifteenth-century Assisian statutes "ne hereditates et successiones ad alios qui non essent de domo ex linea masculina perveniant": *Statutorum* bk. II, rub. 21 (c. 8v of the book). On paraphernalia, see M. Bellomo, *Profili della famiglia italiana nell'età dei comuni* (Catania 1975) 194–208. On the apparently later distinction between paraphernalia and extradotal goods, see J. Kirshner and J. Pluss, "Two Fourteenth-Century Opinions on Dowries,

Let me admit at the start that the only documentary evidence that Pica had property is contained in those records disposing of the properties of persons claiming her as their ascendant. These include goods that may ultimately have been Piccardo's dowry to the friars of San Francesco. Could Piccardo's dowry properties earlier have been the subject of contention between Francis and his father? Might the goods that Francis renounced have ended up belonging after all to the friars through Piccardo's dowry?

The answers to these questions depend on whether or not the term "Piche" or "de Pica" indicates ownership, as I have argued it does. If she owned extradotal property, Pica could readily have willed or allowed Francis the use of any part of it that she did not bestow on Angelo. If on the contrary Angelo's father left his estate to Angelo in his will, neither Francis nor Pietro could have contended for it.[56] But there is no reference to a father in documents regarding Angelo and his children. It is quite possible, ironically, that Piccardo's dowry property had indeed once been disputed between Francis and his father.

The tale of the renunciation of Francis of Assisi lies before us. I have previewed this drama by using notarial documents that do not, it is true, mention or concern Francis's father. By their very silence, however, the same sources have shed some light on Pietro's material interest in Francis's conversion. What could threaten Pietro's status if Francis joined the clergy or otherwise renounced the world? The answer is that since Francis was Pietro's first, and, as appears likely, only son, the boy's desertion of the *saeculum* meant that Pietro's name and estate would end with him. And indeed, there is as little record of Pietro's descendants in the notarial record as there is of Pietro himself. None.

Next, what was the threat to Pietro if Francis, having decided to leave the world, did *not* renounce his rights? The answer is that, even assuming Pietro was the property-holder that tradition says he was, no threat could come to his own estate from Francis as long as this hostile father lived to protect it, and quite as little if he were to die. Entry into any branch of the clergy brought with it submission to ecclesiastical judges, and an effective if not always legal "civil death" or renunciation of access to municipal justice. Even professed monks and beneficed secular clerks found it all but

---

Paraphernalia and Non-Dotal Goods" *Bulletin of Medieval Canon Law* n.s. 9 (1979) 65. The customary right of a daughter to the dowry of her dead mother is mentioned in T. Kuehn, "Women, Marriage, and *Patria Potestas* in Late Medieval Florence," *Tijdschrift voor Rechtsgeschiedenis* 49 (1981) 140–141.

56. Bellomo, *Ricerche* 196, 206ff. For the tenacity with which fifteenth-century and perhaps earlier Assisian statutes would have defended such an inheritance from the father, see *Statutorum* bk. II, rub. 22 (c. 8v of the book).

impossible to bring a civil suit. Francis, as we shall see, intended to become a humble penitent, and he denied the right of local municipal authorities to cite him before them. In doing that, he willy-nilly renounced practically any access to his hostile father's property.[57]

It makes sense that Pietro was concerned with today, not tomorrow, with losses he might suffer while alive, not losses to his eventual estate in death. The confrontation between Pietro and Francis must have been provoked by tangible property that Pica could have given to Francis and thus taken away from Pietro, either immediately or in the event of her death. In the former case the fear could not have been for her dowry, over which Pietro legally disposed until Pica's death. Thus a Pietro concerned with immediate repercussions must have been concerned with other properties Pica had brought to the marriage, ones he could not control as easily. In the case of Pietro's death she could have left property to Francis not as a possession—since he chose a life without property—but for his use in the interest of her soul, much as later sinners would leave property to Piccardo.

Pietro's position was precarious. As a "child of the first bed," Angelo, a youth over whom Pietro had no control, was a formidable competitor for Pica's wealth in the event of his stepfather's or his mother's death. In the person of Francis, however, Pietro was faced with another competitor for the favors of Pica, if one over whom he still exercised some paternal control. Now this son, sickly by all accounts, had been seized by holy madness.[58]

---

57. The notion that a monk renounced his paternal estate by taking religious vows was put forward in the late twelfth and early thirteenth centuries by civilists, and resisted by canonists. Durtelle shows that it had been applied to the friars by the time of the canonist Hostiensis (d. 1271). As regards secular clerks in major orders, Florence as early as 1218 had a law "ut nullus videlicet ad hereditatem paternam clericus admittatur": R. Davidsohn, *Storia di Firenze* 2 (Florence 1956) 78–79; E. Durtelle de Saint-Sauveur, *Recherches sur l'histoire de la théorie de la mort civile des religieux des origines au seizième siècle* (Rennes 1910) 145, 103. By mid-fourteenth century, Assisi had a similar law directed at least against monks, as evidenced in Bartolus: "In civitate Assisii est statutum, quod ingrediens *monasterium* non succedat; an valeat pactum factum cum consanguineis de reservando jure successionis, tempore ingressus? Ad istam questionem examinandam oportet prius videre, an valeat statutum, quod ingrediens monasterium non succedat"; cited ibid. 141. "Fictitious clerks" who (like Francis) claimed the *privilegium fori*, provoked other measures: Italian civil authorities often forbade use of the civil courts upon that claim: see in general L. Prosdocimi, *Il diritto ecclesiastico dello stato di Milano dall'inizio della signoria Viscontea al periodo Tridentino (sec. XIII–XVI)* (Milan 1941) 283–324. My thanks to A. Molho for sharing with me his yet unpublished "Female Religious Professions in Late Medieval Florence." It includes a study of nuns' renunciations in the Quattrocento, entitled "Tamquam Vere Mortue." Unfortunately, M. Bellomo's study of the *pars filii* does not address our situation: *Problemi di diritto familiare nell'età dei comuni: Beni paterni e "pars filii"* (Milan 1968).

58. Manselli, *San Francesco* 57–58.

If Pica were to behave like many other mothers in such circumstances, she would be liable over time to help her son financially, in the hope of securing her own memory and salvation through him.[59] This could only harm the interests of Pietro and Angelo.

The die was cast for this doubly threatened father. Scholars have uniformly seen the renunciation only in terms of patrimony. Yet from Pica's side of the family, things look different. At stake in his son's renunciation of 1206 were the father's posthumous but the mother's present estate. Even the literary tradition will eventually demonstrate it.

59. While our sources never say that Pica helped Francis, Francis exemplarily saw to getting the elderly mother of two of his friars a year's sustenance *because* Francis "called" (2 Celano II, 58) or "said" that "the mother of any [friar] brother was his mother and the mother of all the brothers"; copied by 1 Celano from the Perugian *Legenda*: Habig, *St. Francis* 1029-1030. Further on friars as mothers ibid. 73, 118. Apparently Francis did not call a friar's father his or his fellows' father. See several cases of widows protected by their Dominican sons in the friary of S. Maria Novella in Florence, in my "Magi," in *Church and Community* 75-167. On Christian women supporting the "fathers" of mother church, see J. Goody, *The Development of the Family and Marriage in Europe* (Cambridge 1983) 67-68, 83-94.

2

The Renunciation of Francis According to the Word

The story of the renunciation presented in the standard written sources was composed by males and for males. Its centerpiece, the dramatic conflict between father and son, witnesses that. But why did the two men come to this tragic split? This is a central question, in their handling of which these sources fundamentally disagree.

To be sure, all the sources agree that money lay at the root of the conflict, and none of the authoritative sources suggests that it was Pica's money. But was this money actually a direct cause of Francis's renunciation? That is another matter, and here the sources disagree among themselves. At odds as to whether the money caused the renunciation, they could not agree on whether the money in the story, with its eventual commercial taint, belonged to Pietro, Francis, or God.

BOY FRANCIS

The Life of Francis by friar Tommaso da Celano, written in 1228, is the earliest account (1 Celano). It was done at papal behest in this year of Francis's canonization because shrines to a saint required a biography. Celano was an educated man who had held important administrative posts in the order after joining it around 1215. These positions were mostly in Germany, however, and there is no indication that he had known Francis.[60] This first official Life of the founder is, therefore, a compilation of materials Celano gathered; it does not contain any firsthand experience with Francis, and it

---

60. The sparse materials on Celano are in *AF*, pp. iii-vi. See further F. Casolini's edition of Celano, pp. viii-xxiv; Moorman, *Sources* 61-65; and P. Hermann's Introduction to the English translations of Celano in Habig, *St. Francis* 179-212.

is stereotypically hagiographic. Celano narrates many miracles performed by Francis but makes little direct reference to the disputes that had begun to rage within the order well before Francis's death.

The author begins his account of the events surrounding the renunciation (bk. I, ch. 4–5) with Francis going to the nearby town of Foligno and selling some cloth. In the event, that proves unusual, for all the standard accounts except 1 Celano and the Life of Julian of Speyer (ca. 1235) begin before the trip to Foligno, with a talking crucifix at the church of San Damiano, just outside Assisi, that encourages Francis to raise money.

In 1 Celano, however, Francis did not know what he would do with the receipts from the sale at Foligno. Only on returning to Assisi by way of San Damiano did he then notice that church in disrepair. The young man tried to give his profit to its priest so that he could repair the church and, Celano adds later, feed the poor. Francis then asked and received the priest's permission to reside at the church rather than return home. But the clerk refused to take the money. According to Celano, Francis cared so little for the money that he thereupon discarded it on a windowsill of the church.

Returning after a time to Assisi, Francis was publicly mocked on the way because of his ascetic appearance.[61] His father was humiliated. He seized Francis and chained him at home. When Pietro then left on business, Pica released her son, who promptly returned to San Damiano and his ascetic ways. On returning from his business trip and finding Francis gone again, Pietro decided, in Celano's words, to seize the money (*ad extorquendam pecuniam instigatur*) that Francis had gotten by selling the cloth at Foligno.

Pietro was beside himself, Celano says, but determined as he was, he did succeed in retrieving the money at San Damiano. As a result, Celano says, "the fury of his raging father was a bit extinguished and the thirst of his avarice was somewhat allayed." This change of mood from fury to self-containment happened *before* Pietro first discussed the idea of renunciation with Francis. After their discussion, Pietro went to the bishop together with his son to have Francis "renounce in [the bishop's] hands all his rights, render[ing] everything he had."

---

61. "Cuncti qui noverant eum . . . insanum ac dementem acclamantes, lutum platearum et lapides in ipsum proiciunt. Cernebant eum a pristinis moribus alteratum et carnis maceratione valde confectum"; 1 Celano I, 5. Cf. 'Noti eius . . . eidem miserabiliter insultantes, luto eum et lapidibus impetebant"; *JS*, I, 7. In *TS* (VI, 17) it is the *concives* who do this. Bonaventure's *LM* (II, 2) has citizens doing it, but in his *LMin* (*de conversione*, 6) *iuvenes* do it. Cf. 1 Celano I, 4–6, where Francis is first said to want to repair the church, and then, when his father attacks him, says he had wanted to do that *and* feed the poor. The story from this point on is given in the Appendix.

Since the Latin *extorquere* does not indicate a crime, as "extort" does in English, but only the physical act of grasping, it might not seem that Celano was describing Pietro as taking something that was not his. But by insisting that Pietro was avaricious, the author all but explicitly states that the money at stake belonged to Francis and not to Pietro. Note, however, the open contradiction in the account, indicating that Celano did not know how to deal with a *poverino* who had money at his disposal. On the one hand, Francis wanted to have the church repaired and have the poor fed, and he pressed the money on the priest for that reason. On the other hand, Francis on being refused by the priest valued the money so little that he threw it away—apparently no longer caring whether the roof was repaired or the poor fed. This Franciscan lassitude becomes even more problematical in Celano's second Life, and indeed in all the accounts where the crucifix at San Damiano enjoins Francis to fix the roof, that is, all the accounts after Julian of Speyer. Indeed, in the Three Companions, Francis sells the goods at Foligno precisely to obey that mandate.[62]

There is no indication that friar Julian, from the Rhenish town of Speyer, knew either Celano or Francis, indeed there is little information on Julian at all. He is said to have been a well-regarded teacher of music at the royal court in Paris before 1227, when he is found to be in the order. With the exception of a trip to his native Germany in 1227, and a probable visit to Assisi in 1230, Julian seems to have spent most of his life in Paris, where he held office in the order, died, and was buried. In his own Life of the founder, written between 1232 and 1235, Julian copied or abridged 1 Celano in almost all cases.[63] He tells us nothing new about the whereabouts or status of the money from Francis's sale at the time Pietro took his son before the bishop.

But as is true for so much else regarding Francis's story, the next Life of the founder, by the so-called Three Companions, tells a significantly different, fuller story. For almost a century, the story told by the Three Companions has been the focus of much debate as to its reliability, date, and authorship.[64] Here, however, only the bare outlines of this debate need be sketched.

The work claims to have been compiled at the invitation of the order by a trio of Francis's close friends for the purpose of supplementing Celano's

---

62. Notably, 2 Celano alone does not say that Francis went to Foligno or that he acquired the money by any commercial transaction; for that omission's significance, see below, at note 96.

63. On Julian, see *AF*, pp. xlii–xlviii; Moorman, *Sources* 76–81.

64. In addition to Moorman, *Sources* 68–75, see T. Desbonnets' introduction to his critical edition (*TS*, pp. 38–88), and to the English translation in Habig, *St. Francis* 855–888.

existing biography. That story is certainly suspicious, and yet parts of the work do have the distinct flavor of eyewitnessing. The date of the story seems quite as unproblematical. According to a letter that accompanies the oldest manuscripts, the completed work was submitted to the authorities in 1246. While many scholars have disputed the authenticity of the letter and thus the date of 1246, Théophile Desbonnets, the producer of the recent critical edition, accepts this date. This is a judicious view, because as regards the story of the renunciation, there is no question that in his *second* Life, dated with certainty about 1247, Tommaso da Celano followed the Three Companions, and not vice versa.

On the question of the location and status of the money, the Three Companions prove different from 1 Celano at every turn. Francis threw the money onto the windowsill at San Damiano: that is as much as remains of 1 Celano. The Companions say that once Pietro had decided to do something, he first went to the *town* government, to get *his* money back; that the government summoned Francis to appear before it; that Francis refused to come, telling the messenger that by the grace of God "he has already been made free (*liberum*) and that he is no longer required to obey the consuls, because he wants only to serve God"; that the government then decided not to proceed further, telling Pietro that "since [Francis] has entered the service of God, he is no longer under their *potestas*." In other words, the communal government recognized Francis's assertion of ecclesiastical immunity. The Companions say that Pietro now went to the bishop—but only, be it noted, after being turned down by the government, and still without having gotten his money back.[65]

In this account, Pietro's fury had obviously not been extinguished. There was no calm parley between father and son as in 1 Celano. The father's purpose in going to the bishop was not to have Francis renounce anything, but simply to regain the receipts from the sale at Foligno.

The Three Companions continue. On hearing Pietro's request for the money Francis obviously still controlled, the bishop cited Francis to appear before him to respond to a suit brought by his father; that is, the bishop cited Francis at the instance (as the notaries say, *ad instantiam*) of his father, and not *ex officio*. Francis gladly came (and perforce, for having refused civil jurisdiction, he had no choice but to appear in episcopal curia). When Francis appeared, the bishop told him that if he wanted to serve God—that is, maintain the clerical or penitential immunity that the bishop had recog-

---

65. See below, note 96, on the conflicting evidence of where the money actually was. On Francis's entry into the clergy, see V. da Clusone, "Quando ebbe la tonsura S. Francesco d'Assisi?", *Italia Francescana* 9 (1934) 15–28.

nized in the act of citing him to appear—he would have to render the money. It could not be used to rebuild the church because, said the bishop, "it was perhaps unjustly acquired," *and* because Pietro was sinning, seemingly by being beside himself with anger. In this account, Francis then returned the money to his father in the presence of the bishop.

The Three Companions differ from 1 Celano up till now in many respects. But two points are central in the present context. First, the Three Companions indicate that the money was on Francis's person when he appeared before the bishop. Remember that in 1 Celano, Pietro had already regained his money on his own, and thus went to the bishop only to have his son renounce inheritance. Second, in the Three Companions the bishop is a judge. He took Francis under his protection by putting his cloak over him. That is, he recognized Francis's clerical status. But just before that action, he had rendered two judgments. First, he opined that the money in question was perhaps unjustly acquired. Second, he judged that the money could not be applied to church purposes because it was perhaps unjustly acquired and because Pietro would continue to sin if it was not returned to him. All this is absent from 1 Celano. The Three Companions are said to have supplemented 1 Celano. As regards the renunciation, however, they rewrote it.

Celano penned his second Life of Francis (2 Celano) around 1247, and while he like the Companions said he only meant to supplement 1 Celano, we should not be taken in by the pious ruse.[66] Celano did nothing less than discard his earlier account and accept that of the Three Companions, if in abbreviated form. Celano too now says that Francis went to the court of the bishop with the money; Pietro had not already retrieved it. Second, Francis handed it over to Pietro once the bishop had ruled, in Celano's words, that "it was not lawful to spend anything for sacred uses that had been gotten unlawfully" (Celano's second *vita* does not cite Pietro's sin of anger as a reason for Francis to return the money, as had the Companions). I shall return to these episcopal rulings. What is important here is that both Celano and the Three Companions now agreed that the renunciation was intimately tied to retrieving money, and that retrieval was accomplished pursuant to at least one legal judgment on the part of the ordinary. The authors' agreement on these points may in turn hint at the legal condition of Francis at this point.

---

66. F. De Beer was not; *Conversion*. Nor was a reviewer of De Beer: G. Miccoli, "Conversione" 776–777. On the relation of both stories to 1 Celano, see P. Hermann in Habig, *St. Francis* 186–189.

FRANCIS AT TWENTY-FIVE

In his first Life, Celano (I, 2) says that Francis lived the good life until he was twenty-five years of age. Scholars have not asked why this author adopted twenty-five as the age of Francis's renunciation or conversion, but students of the law will understand my interest in this detail. The question is significant because of the disagreement over whether Francis sold his own goods or his father's and thus retained his own money or someone else's. After all, the biblical dicta all said that in order to be perfect, one should sell one's own goods, not a father's!

In the abstract, that disagreement can be understood quite apart from the question of age. For example, a classic legal *questio* of the time posited a situation in which a son increased the value of goods a father assigned him, and then simply asked: did the father or the son own the increase of that *peculium profectitium*? Opinions differed, but one key ingredient of any answer was whether the property in question increased passively (*simpliciter*), in Bartolus's words, or "through the industry of the son" (*ex industria filii*). Let us assume for a moment that the cloth Francis took to Foligno was Pietro's. Clearly, Francis had worked to sell it, and so he might consider any profit his own property.[67]

But it cannot be assumed that the cloth *was* Pietro's. By indicating that Francis was twenty-five years old, Celano means to make age relevant. For twenty-five was the legal age of majority. Thus it was one thing for a person who had passed that age (when one could become a priest, for example) to take goods and sell them, and another matter for a person who was below that age to do so. What those differences were are not always clear, for the legal effect of majority in the Middle Ages has not been studied as carefully as has the institution of emancipation.[68]

---

67. For details, see Bellomo, *Profili* 212–215.

68. Neither M. Bellomo ("Emancipazione [dir. interm.]", *Enciclopedia del diritto* 14 [Milan 1965] 809–818) nor T. Kuehn (*Emancipation in Late Medieval Florence* [New Brunswick 1982]) gives majority sufficient attention. Further, both explain that emancipation terminated *patria potestas*, but they say nothing about the relation of majority or emancipation to entry into the clergy or the status of penitent; see esp. Kuehn, *Emancipation* 21–22, 32–33, 49–50, 87. For majority in traditional Benedictine monasticism, see the views of Leclercq cited in T. Fry, ed., *RB 1980: the Rule of St. Benedict in Latin and English with Notes* (Collegeville 1981) 271. Municipal statutes show that, in practice, majority made a difference, by emphasizing that a layman of this period might remain unemancipated past majority. For example, "statuimus . . . observanandum in filio familias, etiam maiore viginti quinque annis": statutes of Reggio Emilia (1265-1273), cited with other such formulations in Bellomo, *Problemi* 3–4. On the significance of age twenty-five in fifteenth-century Assisi, and perhaps earlier, see above, at note 45. The legal category of adulthood is also important to mention, for *TS* (I, 2) says that Francis "postquam fuit adultus . . . , artem patris id est negociationem exercuit"; a sixteenth-century

The rite of emancipation is just as relevant to our examination. It was not tied to a specific age as was majority. A child might be emancipated. Then again, a grown man might never be emancipated. By this rite, a father publicly ended his child's submission to the *patria potestas*. The emancipated person gained certain rights to make contracts, and both parties limited their responsibilities for each other's debts. To signify the child's new legal status, the father usually gave some gift of property to the child.

It would be wrong to assume that the emancipator was always in a position of strength. My review of the contexts of emancipation has turned up several where the father was financially weak when he freed his child: the emancipation actually disadvantaged the child to the father's benefit, such as in those several Italian judicial venues where fathers emancipated sons or daughters on the condition that they promptly renounce their rights to parental property.

Could Francis's renunciation have come about in such a circumstance, or have been imagined by contemporaries in such a context? The closest I can come to a positive answer in this regard is by showing that at the end of the fifteenth century, Florentine males about to profess in religious orders were being emancipated and renouncing simultaneously.[69] But be that as it may, it was obviously one thing for a son who had been legally emancipated or "freed" by and from his father to behave as Francis and quite another if he had not gone through that formal separation from the *patria potestas*.

Friars rather than lawyers though they were, our sources certainly knew all this, for questions of age, emancipation, and majority affected one's right to enter the religious life and one's resources in doing so. Thus, though the Three Companions were certainly referring (as had 1 Celano)

---

variant adds: "cioè d'anni XIIII": *Leggenda di San Francesco d'Ascesi scritta dalli suoi compagni che tutt'hora conversavano con lui*, ed. S. Melchiorri (Recanati 1856) 3. But in fifteenth-century Florence, adulthood was reached at eighteen, the age of youth only later: Trexler, *Public Life* 388. Kuehn, *Emancipation* 208, thinks that in the Florentine sources, reference to the adult age of eighteen means "that all legal capacities were available without recourse to guardianship."

69. See these 1499 and 1507 cases in *Archivio di Stato, Firenze, Carte Strozziane* IV, 353, ff. 3v, 6v, kindly brought to my attention by C. Klapisch-Zuber. The 1499 case is especially interesting because it specifies that the emancipation and renunciation would only take effect if they were followed by monastic profession. See further the intriguing, undated Sienese *consilium* described by Kuehn, *Emancipation* 136: one messer Jacopo, claiming he had not renounced, apparently argued that a notary could not combine an act of renunciation and one of emancipation in the same record. The jurisprudent, however, ruled that the notary had acted correctly in doing so. See also cases of women being emancipated while renouncing their rights to their mother's dowry: Kuehn, "Women" 140–141. I consulted *Pauli Gallerati . . . De Renuntiationibus Tractatus* 1–3 (Geneva 1678), esp. ch. 25 of tome 2 (pp. 97ff), without encountering a renunciation comparable to Francis's situation of renouncing the world without entering a religious order. A study of earlier *consilia* might be fruitful.

to Francis's freedom from the *saeculum* when they had him proclaim his freedom from the lay government,[70] they perhaps also meant to suggest that God the Father had emancipated Francis whereas Pietro had refused to. Emancipation, I repeat, meant the end of *patria potestas*. In the present case, it seems to have proceeded in two steps. First, Francis denied the *potestas* of the communal fathers. Then he claimed clerical status by denying his father's *potestas* simultaneously.[71] Yet the son kept the father's money. By the Three Companions' account, Francis clearly thought that there came a point in one's life when one could give to the church or to the poor money that belonged to one's father.

In all cases, the vagueness of the sources will frustrate the student trying to grasp the legal implications of the Francis story. But here, I think, we have come to the crux of the matter. If we try to explain the narrative conflict over the location of the money at the time of the renunciation, the Three Companions urge us to weigh Francis's legal status. That same legal status also comes to the foreground if we are to evaluate Francis's, nay anyone's, decision to expend money on church fabrics or on the poor. The "poor" includes, of course, the institutionally poor descendants of the holy man of Assisi. These Lives of Francis were, after all, exempla for future converts to and lay supporters of the order. Obviously, the matter of who had a right to give money to the church or to the poor was a matter of utmost importance to the young Franciscan order, and to the hagiographers.

But had Francis actually intended to give money from his Foligno sale to the poor, or was it meant solely for rebuilding the church? Contemporaries were well aware of the difference: it was one thing to help the poor and another to spend money on physical plant. From its beginnings, critics inside and outside the order declaimed against the Franciscans' large churches, and the order had plenty of enemies who disputed Francis's sanctity and saw him as just one more avaricious man of God.[72] For an order

---

70. Francis was at a certain point "not yet freed from the cords of vanity": 1 Celano I, 2. Cf. a fourteenth-century northern manuscript paraphrasing TS: "respondit se ad altius fori esse obligatum nec tenebatur coram consulibus respondere"; Fierens, "Question franciscaine" 301.

71. Kuehn, *Emancipation* does not mention the nexus between a father, and a commune as father, or of the clergy as the *communis patria*; on this, see G. Post, "Two Notes on Nationalism in the Middle Ages," *Traditio* 9 (1953) 286-289; E. Kantorowicz, *The King's Two Bodies* (Princeton 1957) 211, 232-272 (esp. 234, 258), 304, 476. Also my *Public Life* 29, on males of political age and family never saying they were "governed" by the commune.

72. Before 1289, a clerical preacher denounced Francis to his flock as a "rusticus vilis et maledictus mercator cupidus . . . , sanctus numquam": A. Vauchez, "Les stigmates de Saint François et leurs détracteurs dans les derniers siècles du moyen âge," *Mélanges d'archéologie et d'histoire* 80 (1968) 614. For declamations against Franciscan church building, see Moorman, *History* 119, 197, 199.

of institutionally poor men trying simultaneously to protect its reputation, attract funds, and win converts, the question of Francis's intention at this point was thus no small matter. As Bonaventure now read the sources while preparing to pen his own biography of the founder, he could not avoid noticing how troubling this question had already been for his predecessors, and how stark his own choice was. On the one hand there was the Francis who thought of the poor. That Francis followed the biblical injunction, "Sell everything you have and give [the proceeds] to the poor" (Matt. 19.21). On the other there was a possibly niggardly, not to say vainglorious youth who, by obeying the crucifix, would build a monument to himself.

Indeed, on closer inspection we can see that the choice between the two Francises was actually present in the very different accounts of 1 Celano and Julian of Speyer, before the crucifix ever entered the story. Recall that Celano had mentioned Francis's desire to feed the poor from the Foligno money only as an afterthought. Yet then, obviously troubled by the emphasis he had placed on Francis's plans to expend the money on the church fabric, Celano cautioned his readers that Francis only meant to rebuild an old church, not to make a new one. Indirectly, this formulation reemphasized feeding the poor and warned his brothers in the order not to build new churches.[73]

Otherwise a loyal follower of Celano in the renunciation story, Julian of Speyer apparently did not find this part of the account compelling or edifying. Though still without the talking crucifix, which would emerge only in the Three Companions, this author did modify Celano's hero's intent. Julian has Francis return from Foligno having already made up his mind how he was going to use the money. Francis intended it, he says, "for the pious . . . uses of the poor, and as pious offerings for other necessities."[74] Julian—alone in this respect—thus placed Francis's concern for the poor first, while the repair of the church became simply "another necessity." The contrast between this account and that of 1 Celano could not be clearer. For Julian of Speyer, this exemplary man thought first about the poor and only later about the physical plant.

But if both early sources had room for the poor at some point in their account, the two subsequent authorities have none at all. Now the crucifix of San Damiano specifically orders a new roof over its head. *Neither the*

---

73. "Illamque non de novo facere tentat, sed veterem reparat, vetustam resarcit; non fundamentum evellit, sed super illud aedificat, praerogativam, licet ignorans, semper reservans Christo: *Fundamentum enim aliud nemo potest ponere, praeter id quod positum est, quod est Christus Iesus*": I, 8. An alternate reading would be that Celano was subtly condemning heresies, but the passage certainly glosses Francis's testament, wherein the saint had forbidden "temples of large dimensions and richly decorated": A. Chastel, *Italian Art* (New York 1963) 88.

74. "Piis illam pauperum usibus, piis aliarum necessitatum obsequiis": *JS*, I, 6.

Three Companions nor *2 Celano* makes any mention of the poor. In both accounts the bishop, charged with maintaining churches, will rule *only* on the legality of Francis applying the money for that purpose.

The significance of this omission of any reference to the poor belies less an indifference to the impoverished laity than to claims that the Franciscan order and its members were poor by definition. I noted earlier that many persons thought of the Franciscans as poor by institutional definition. Would a later Franciscan postulant fulfill Jesus' admonition to give all to the poor by giving to the Franciscan order? This omission in the Francis story of the Companions and 2 Celano might have loaned credence to this idea.

At a minimum, then, two fundamental questions were in play: first, the relative importance of building churches as against helping the poor, and second, the definition of "the poor."

THE FRANCIS OF BONAVENTURE

The flexibility of Tommaso da Celano in discarding his previous attempt and adopting the Three Companions' version was not to Bonaventura da Bagnoregio's liking. Neither were the threatening implications of the story now told by Celano and the Three Companions. The troubled conditions of the order at the time the so-called Seraphic Doctor assumed its generalship in 1257 are well known. The Franciscans were already close to being in schism. The strict Spirituals, as they would be called, adhered to the pristine ideals of Francis regarding poverty. For example, they preferred Francis's so-called first rule, which said that postulants had to renounce everything they had before being accepted, to the so-called second rule, which provided entry to postulants who were unable to renounce property, as long as they showed good intentions in that regard.[75] Such evasions allowed the order to use such properties if not to possess them, and the order indeed undertook an orgy of church building and ornamentation in the years before Bonaventure assumed his office. The Conventuals, to use their later name, tended to accept the use if not the ownership of property, and many other practices that were anathema to the Spirituals, as the price of the order's growth.

---

75. Compare, from ch. 2 of the first rule, "Omnia sua vendat et ea omnia pauperibus studeat erogare," to the comparable passage of ch. 2 in the second rule: "Vendant omnia sua et ea studeant pauperibus erogare. Quod si facere non potuerint, sufficit eis bona voluntas": K. Esser, ed., *Die Opuscula des Hl. Franziskus von Assisi. Neue textkritische Edition* (Grottaferrata 1976), respectively 378, 367. See Moorman's comment on the change in rule 2: *History* 58. Also M. Lambert, *Franciscan Poverty* (London 1961), chs. 4 and 5. The practical implications of this modification are worked out in *Peter Olivi's Rule Commentary*, ed. D. Flood (Wiesbaden 1972) 126–127.

The Spirituals were suspected of heresies associated with the name of Joachim of Flore, including the prediction that a group of strict poor men would renew religion. For their part, the so-called lax minister generals were viewed by the strict Mendicants as recreating the biblical plagues. Now in chapter, the friars looked to their minister general Bonaventure to resolve such violent debates, in part by restudying Francis's life. Written between 1260 and 1263 on the request of the order, Bonaventure's Life was intended to be definitive, and in adopting it in 1266, the chapter general of the order concurrently ordered all other Lives destroyed.

As minister general, Bonaventure understood that to procure the desired peace, his Francis had to be a model, not only for a majority of the brothers but for the *saeculum* as well, especially for those laymen who wanted to join the order.[76] What has not been examined in the study of Bonaventure's Life is the impact of these forces upon the story of the renunciation.

To create this model founder, Bonaventure bypassed 2 Celano and the Three Companions, obviously because they did not contribute to his goal, and returned to Celano's first Life of 1228 and to Julian of Speyer's similar Life of about 1235. He adopted from the tradition of the Three Companions only their story about the talking crucifix. Here is the thrust of his *vita*: Bonaventure wanted the world and the order to remember, first, the crucifix commanding Francis to sell *his* goods at Foligno to finance a new roof over its head; second, a boy who did think of the poor; third, an avaricious father whose ire had been assuaged by his finding the money before the bishop became involved; fourth, a son who appeared in curia unencumbered and untainted with money that might itself have been tainted; fifth, a Francis who came to the bishop purely for the purpose of renouncing his inheritance as his father wished him to do. Sixth and last, Bonaventure would seek to immortalize a passive bishop who did not cite Francis to appear and who made no legal judgments about Franciscan money.

Now for a more detailed picture. As regards the background to the renunciation, there are only two small variations between Bonaventure's account and that of 1 Celano, which I shall only note for now. First, Bonaventure wanted to leave no doubt that the repairs the crucifix ordered Francis to make to the roof of San Damiano were predominantly symbolic in nature: the crucifix meant for Francis to repair the universal church. Second

---

76. See R. Manselli's overview of "Bonaventura di Bagnoregio," *Dizionario biografico degli Italiani* 11 (Rome 1969) 612–619. On the troubles in his time, Moorman, *History* 140–155. Through the works of Bonaventure's contemporary, the canonist Hostiensis (d. 1271), all the crucial inheritance questions regarding Franciscans were already on the table: Durtelle de Saint-Sauveur, *Recherches* 102–103.

and more relevant to our discourse at this point, 1 Celano and Julian of Speyer had portrayed Pietro wanting Francis to render up everything, "renouncing in the [bishop's hands] all his rights." But Bonaventure says that Pietro wanted Francis "to renounce in [the bishop's] hands all *paternal* rights and to render everything he had."[77] Central as this variant will prove to be, at this point I insist only upon the fact that in Bonaventure's official Life of Francis, the money problem was solved before the renunciation. Cash is absent from the episcopal curia.

RENUNCIATIONS

Having reviewed the background to the renunciation in the five early accounts, we can comprehend the differences in their descriptions of the event itself. In 1 Celano, Julian of Speyer, and Bonaventure, Francis arrived in curia with the purpose of renouncing. He no sooner came before the bishop than he stripped himself of all his clothes, "restituting them to his father." Bonaventure then adds that once Francis had stripped, he said, "Up until now I called you my terrestrial father, but now more surely I can say: 'Our father who art in heaven.'"

That small twist had also appeared in the Three Companions and 2 Celano, but for the rest, those sources tell the story differently. In the accounts of the Companions and 2 Celano, Francis came to court with coins in hand. The renunciation was *Francis's* idea *after* the bishop persuaded the boy that the money had to be turned over. The bishop's argument will be analyzed shortly. But here is the subsequent text of the Three Companions, translated from the Latin in the Appendix. Francis speaks:

> "Not only do I want to render the money to him, which belongs to him, with a happy spirit, but also the clothes, which belong to him." And entering the room of the bishop, he removed all his clothes, which belonged to [Pietro], and placed the money over them in the presence of the bishop and his father and some bystanders. And then, naked, he went outside and said: "Hear and understand everything. Up

---

77. Bonaventure reformulated his words in his *LMin* (*de conversione*, 7): "ut episcopum civitatis una secum adiret: eiusque renunciaret in manibus hereditario iuri paternarum omnium facultatum." Obviously, this formulation was not new in a fourteenth-century northern manuscript, as Fierens says it was: "Question" 301–302. Curiously, the reference to paternal goods did not originate with Bonaventure. The English monk Roger of Wendover (d. 1236) had already zeroed in on the father's goods: "sed quod mente conceperat, ut liberius opere compleret, hereditatem paternam non modicam cum cunctis seculi oblectamentis despiciens, cucullam et cilicium induit, calciamenta deposuit": *The Flowers of History* 2 (London 1887) 328. I have seen no suggestion, however, that the often unreliable Roger was known to the mainstream writers. Roger's precedence on this score remains an oddity to me.

till now I called only Pietro di Bernardone 'father.' But because I propose to serve God, I render to him [Pietro] the money, which has bothered him, and all the clothes I had from his possessions. I want only to say: 'Our father, who is in heaven,' [and] not: 'Father Pietro di Bernardone'."

Bonaventure obviously adopted from the Companions Francis's oration changing fathers because he wanted the renunciation to be the single centerpiece or symbolic act marking Francis's passage from the world to the spirit. It is true that the Three Companions also stressed this moment as one of conversion, but they had not written with Bonaventure's teleology in mind. The Companions do not intimate that Francis came to the episcopal palace with any other intention than to hold onto the money. Warned by the bishop to give it up or lose his immunity, Francis in the Companions' account rendered the money *and then* ripped off his clothes.[78] Already emancipated of the money, the Francis of Bonaventure, on the other hand, is predestined, and no episcopal judgments are necessary. Reading between the lines, it is clear that the Francis of the now-forbidden tradition of the Companions left the world to spite Pietro, after being warned by the prelate that he could not both emancipate himself *and* give to the church the money he had earned off his father's goods before that emancipation.

Yet Bonaventure's closing act is decorous, and lacks any of the violence that had marked Pietro's and Francis's previous relations. Bonaventure follows 1 Celano in saying nothing of the father's comportment in curia; both note only that Pietro arrived with his ire assuaged. The Three Companions on the contrary portray a father still agitated precisely because he still wanted his money. Seated during the son's whole performance, the angry father in this account then stood up. Pietro had come only to get his money back, but Francis had shown ultimate spite and disowned his father. Without turning on the inspired youth, Pietro gathered up the clothes and money that Francis had thrown on the ground, and walked away.

EXCHANGING MONEY

In reviewing the tradition to this point, I have suggested that the several writers obeyed different motives in shaping their accounts. In the light of

---

78. While all writers say he was left nude, only 1 Celano, JS, and Bonaventure add the phrase "including his trousers" (*femuralia*), and in the first and last Italian paintings of the scene (figs. 1 and 20), Francis wears underpants. In fact, the word "nude" at this time sometimes meant only barechested. On the topos of the nude following Christ, see M. Bernards, "Nudus nudum Christum sequi," *Wissenschaft und Weisheit* 14 (1951) 148-151. Precedents for Francis's act are recorded in Weinstein and Bell, *Saints and Society* 50. On the link between undressing and renunciation in traditional monasticism, see A. de Vogüé, ed., *La règle de Saint Benoit* 6 (Paris 1971) 957.

modern hagiographical studies, this is hardly surprising.[79] Each writer saw Francis in terms of what was important to the order at the time he wrote. At the beginning, Francis had only to be proved a saint who would inspire other individuals, and that always makes for effortless storytelling. In an early sermon, for example, a preacher told his audience that Francis gave everything away the minute God ordered him to, and thus was the perfect example for others.[80] He did not bother with details.

Yet in the end, writers, if not preachers, had to edify an established order of poor men by meliorating its internal conflicts, and they had to do it in such a way that the *saeculum* would continue to support the Franciscans in their poverty. The story of the status of the money from Foligno was, it appears, a touchstone in this changing history. Still, Francis did not renounce to enter an established order, and so his story is not the best one for me to show how the dynamics of narrative were affected by an order's changing needs. Who can imitate a father? Francis was the hero-founder whose very essence depended on standing alone, on being disorderly, and he could better be presented to readers as a stigmatized martyr to be mourned by the guilty than as a brother to be imitated.[81]

---

79. See e.g., the introduction to Weinstein and Bell's *Saints and Society*. I traced the manipulation of one Franciscan's life over time (Martin of Valencia) in "Alla destra di Dio. Organizzazione della vita attraverso i santi morti in Nuova Spagna," *Church and Community* 515–516.

80. "Beatus Franciscus statim, ut audivit vocem Dei, cuncta dimisit, in tantum, ut nec filum vestimenti ad cooperiendam nuditatem sibi reservaverit; immo, sicut omnia interius contemp-serat, sic omnia exterius dimittebat. Per hunc etiam modum qui vult esse perfectus discipulus Christi *vadat et vendat* omnia, *quae habet, et det pauperibus*": Bonaventure, *Opera omnia* 9.591. I. Brady dismissed G. Abate's doubt about Bonaventure's authorship of this sermon and (for me, unpersuasively) reaffirmed that attribution, claiming it was delivered on 4 October 1255: Brady, "The Authenticity of Two Sermons of Saint Bonaventure," *Franciscan Studies* 28 (1968) 4–13; "St. Bonaventure's Sermons on Saint Francis," *Franziskanische Studien* 58 (1976) 137–140. Brady himself could find nothing in the sermon about Francis that evoked words or concepts in Bonaventure's genuine writings about the saint's life, including the *Legenda maior* of 1263.

However, this sermon about Francis's life, emphasizing as it does his giving to the poor just before the renunciation, may date even before 1255, perhaps before 1246/47. The only source Brady found for the preacher's remarks about Francis was Julian of Speyer, writing ca. 1235. As noted earlier, it was precisely Julian who insisted that Francis meant from the start to give to the poor, while the Companions and 2 Celano, writing ca. 1246/47, make no reference to Francis giving to the poor; see above, at note 74. For the other two characterizations of Francis by this preacher, see below, at notes 85 and 105.

81. On Francis as martyr, see 1 Celano II, 7. Since in his renunciation—before a bishop, not an abbot—Francis was not entering an order, contemporary monastic profession offers little by way of useful comparisons. Nor, *pace* de Vogüé, does the Benedictine rule even use the word renunciation; cf., A. de Vogüé, *The Rule of Saint Benedict. A Doctrinal and Spiritual Com-*

The model for those joining the Franciscan order, on the contrary, was to be fra Bernardo of Quintavalle, the first follower of Francis or, better said, the second member of the embryonic order. In his first Life, Tommaso da Celano unmistakably compares the conversion of Bernardo to that of Francis, and this comparison justifies our following Bernardo in the later Lives. He proves a template of Francis, but one who reflects the difference between a hero-founder and a Franciscan follower.

Tommaso da Celano uses Bernardo to tell people how to join the Franciscan order. This Bernardo was an Assisian who gave haven to "the holy father" Francis in his home after Francis had broken with his father. He became so impressed with Francis's holiness that he decided to join him. The characterization of Francis as father probably indicates that Celano thought of Bernardo as being of Francis's age or younger. Bernardo was definitely well-to-do, since he served Celano as *the* example among the early converts who was not "simple." His story thus served to encourage rich young men to join the order. This was no mean trick in any case, and especially unusual among the Franciscans.[82] Celano's strategy at this point was to target a select few who might be recruited.

This insight enables us to appreciate Celano's comparison of Bernardo to Francis. Celano says that, having decided to convert, Bernardo followed the gospel and "sold all his goods and gave the money to the poor, *though not to his parents*." "His conversion," Celano observes shortly after, "was a model to others in the manner of selling one's possessions and giving them to the poor."[83] Was 1 Celano implying that Francis had been forced to return

---

mentary (Kalamazoo 1983) 209–227 ("The Renunciation of Property"). Other rules, alas forgotten in this age, are more helpful for comparisons. For the Pacomian rule, see Fry, *Rule of St. Benedict* 437–438; and see especially L. Eberle, ed., *The Rule of the Master* (Kalamazoo 1977) 254, 270–271. Also J. Lynch, *Simoniacal Entry into Religious Life from 1000 to 1260* (Columbus 1976), pp. xiii, xvi. On the actual practice of Benedictine renunciation in later centuries, see below, at note 129. The classical, late medieval treatise on the legal status of the Franciscans is by Bartolus: see the references in Durtelle de Saint-Sauveur, *Recherches* 104–105.

82. On the anti-religious character of young men, and the resulting awe when they converted, see Trexler, *Public Life* 388–389. See 1 Celano I, 1, a tirade against today's evil parents, including Pietro and Pica, and today's evil young people, including the pre-converted Francis. Objective evidence on the age of entering Franciscans is hard to come by, but some early Franciscan social profiles are offered in J. Freed, *The Friars and German Society in the Thirteenth Century* (Cambridge, Mass. 1977) 109–134, esp. 121–122. As for social status, the Franciscans notoriously recruited from lower levels than the Dominicans. Contemporaries used the topos of "better people" joining the order, as they did "youth," to demonstrate that the order was wanted by God: C. Esser, *Origins of the Franciscan Order* (Chicago 1970) 32.

83. "Accelerat proinde vendere omnia sua et pauperibus, non parentibus, elargitus est ea . . . . Eius namque ad Deum conversio forma exstitit convertendis in venditione et elargitione pauperum": 1 Celano I, 10. Note that Celano thus also excludes giving goods to churches. In

his goods to his parents? At the very least, he intimated that those who now joined the young order should, on the contrary, give their goods to the poor.

The Franciscans, of course, were among the poor, so Celano could hardly avoid reckoning that this emulable procedure of rich young men would help the order grow. No one could have known in 1228 that the order would grow rich quite apart from dowries from joiners. I am suggesting, in short, that 1 Celano was praising Bernardo for having given his wealth, in part at least, to the mendicant friars. Certainly, there were those who from the beginning resented postulants who by hook or crook passed their wealth to some such "poor" Franciscans who were not poor.

But the ambivalence was seemingly unavoidable, even in telling Bernardo's story. In the *Actus* of Francis written by Ugolino Boniscambi between 1327 and 1342, Bernardo was told by a missal "to give everything to the poor." The author thought Bernardo had done that when he "liberally and of his own free will gave [his wealth] to widows, to orphans, to pilgrims, *and to the servants of God.*"[84]

The historians who followed 1 Celano remarkably transformed the figure of Bernardo, reflecting the growth in the order's power and wealth. This transformation begins with one central fact: none of the subsequent Lives intimated to wealthy converts that they should not give their wealth to their parents or relatives. The admonition of Luke (14.26), that to follow Jesus one must hate one's parents, disappears from Francis's second rule in 1223. The days of building the order through conflict with lay relatives were past.[85] The days of relying on lay philanthropy *and* on converts to the

---

2 Celano II, 49, there is a story of Francis condemning a man who, wanting to follow Francis, "ductus amore carnali, sua suis dispersit, nihilque pauperibus"; 1 Celano's formulation just before the cited passage, to the effect that Bernardo followed Francis *ad mercandum regnum caelorum*, suggests that the author thought the convert a merchant. See Bernardo's miracles in *AF*, 3, pp. 34–45.

84. My italics: "Liberaliter et di sua spontana volontà dandone a vedove, a orfani, e a pellegrini et a servi di dio": B. Bughetti, "Una parziale nuova traduzione degli *Actus* accoppiata ad alcuni capitoli dei *Fioretti*," *Archivum Franciscanum Historicum* 21 (1928) 540. On the tradition of mendicants taking goods "ut vendant et se alant," see Durtelle de Sainte-Sauveur, *Recherches* 103, 106. Bernardo's problem of disposing of his wealth obviously refers directly to the ancient Benedictine problematic. See de Vogüé, *Règle* 6.955; Lynch, *Simoniacal Entry*, p. xvi. The main difference between monasteries and convents quickly became that while neither's inhabitants could possess *ut singuli*, the friars could also not possess *in communi*: Durtelle de Sainte-Sauveur, *Recherches* 101–107.

85. Significantly, the sermon on Francis (wrongly?) attributed to Bonaventure (see above, note 80) does cite the Luke passage, and then states uniquely: "Hoc videns, beatus Franciscus patrem et matrem odivit, dum, affectionis carnalis vinculo fracto, eos penitus dereliquit": Bonaventure, *Opera omnia* 9.591. I cannot find these words or sentiments in any other sources, least of all in Bonaventure.

order from the successful artisan and merchant class, as well as on those who joined the order on their deathbed, were abuilding. The Three Companions now speak of a *Lord* Bernardo who had been rich for many years. He was, in short, an older, independent man and, as the title *dominus* indicates, not a (usuring) merchant but a knight or judge of "great edification" or standing in the community whose conversion would obviously bring with it no conflict with relatives over wealth.[86]

Now it was simply a question of what Bernardo should do with his money. In the Three Companions, Bernardo revealed to Francis his desire to follow him, and put to the holy youth a hypothetical question. What should a man do who had held (*tenuisset*) the properties of a lord for years, but now wanted to be rid of them? Francis immediately said that that person should return such properties to their lord. Francis, the Three Companions allow us to infer, had done the same. When Bernardo now said that he had gotten his goods from God—perhaps meaning by inheritance but more probably meaning that he had earned them himself—Francis proved, by his famous triple opening of the missal, that Bernardo should give them to the poor as to God. Bernard did just that, and together he and Francis formed the "society" that would become the Franciscan order.[87]

Thus whereas in his early *vita* Celano had the cohort Bernardo become a "needed companion and a faithful friend," the Three Companions converted Bernardo into an older man whose "edification" was central to the very legitimacy of the order. The legitimation of religious groups by the adhesion to them of mature men of high social status is a topos known to all medievalists.[88]

In his second Life (I, 10), Celano did what he had done with Francis's renunciation: he dismissed his early account, and totally took on the Companions' version. In his turn, Bonaventure accepted as he found it the notion

---

86. "Dominus Bernardus erat homo aedificationis magnae . . . quis multa . . . tenuisset per multos annos": *TS*, VIII, 27-28. The later *Actus* elaborates upon the new Bernardo: "Era de' notabili huomini e gentile della città d'Ascesy e savissimo huomo, et ogne gente della terra andava a llui per consiglio": Bughetti, "Una parziale nuovo traduzione" 538.

87. The scenario applied to a person who had held "multa vel pauca" (cf., note 82), but obviously *dominus* Bernardo had *multa*, as 1 Celano had said. "Beatus Franciscus respondit quod ea domino suo deberet reddere a quo eadem recepisset. . . . Beatus ergo Franciscus . . . dixit . . . : 'Fratres, haec est vita et regula nostra et omnium qui voluerint nostrae societati coniungi' ": *TS*, VIII, 28-29.

88. It is no accident, for example, that while the simple St. Anthony of Padua became the Franciscan saint par excellence of preaching, Louis of Anjou, the son of a king, became the model of poverty: D. Blume, *Wandmalerei als Ordenspropaganda. Bildprogramme im Chorbereich Franziskanischer Konvente Italiens bis zur Mitte des 14. Jahrhunderts* (Worms 1983) 109. On recruitment strategies in Florence once the order was established, see J. Newton, "Poverty and Charity in Late Medieval Florence" (diss. in progress: Brown University), ch. 3.

that Bernardo was of "venerable" station and thus of advanced age, implying by the term "venerable" alone that Bernardo was also wealthy. Bonaventure told the same story of opening the book, but crucially, he eliminated the Three Companions' and 2 Celano's story of Bernardo's hypothetical question about the proper recipient of goods: the goods of any new member of their Franciscan society would be given to the poor, and that was that.[89]

The tale of Bernardo's conversion reveals the changing state of the order, and the greater distance from the founder. Nowhere in these accounts is there emphasis on Bernardo's renunciation of his inheritance, present or future. The story is about a one-time surrender of property in hand. From a rich cohort who had rightly given his goods to the poor as Francis had not been allowed to, Bernardo in the Three Companions became an older pillar of the community who said that people who had their own money owed everything to God, and should ideally restitute that wealth to God, as Francis had been deprived of doing because of his dependence or lack of emancipation from his father. Bonaventure in turn eliminated all talk of restitution, and thus of reference to Francis. Francis's renunciation story was one thing; the ideal of a society was another.

Tainted Money

And yet, in the process of retelling *Francis's* story, Bonaventure changed three other quite fundamental details. First, he excised from the tale the bishop as judge. Second, while Francis remained a person who liked to build churches, by eliminating the bishop as judge Bonaventure reduced the legal importance of Francis's giving money for church fabrics that were under the control of the bishop's secular clergy, and replaced this problem with the injunction that those who entered *the order* must give everything to "the poor"—who, if they were Franciscans, might themselves build churches.

Finally, determined to rob the bishop of his judicial relevance to Franciscan operations, Bonaventure eliminated from the *vita* tradition the question that had been so central to the Three Companions and to 2 Celano: the question of "badly earned goods." For it was always the bishop who had the ultimate duty to determine if goods were badly earned, and we have seen that the order, yes even Francis's own nephew Piccardo, was already

---

89. "Coeperunt ipsius exemplo viri quidam ad poenitentiam animari. . . . Primus exstitit venerabilis vir Bernardus. . . . 'Haec est,' ait vir sanctus, 'vita et regula nostra omniumque, qui nostrae voluerint societati coniungi'": *LM*, III, 3. Note the link between advanced age (*venerabilis*) and becoming a brother *de penitentia*.

in Bonaventure's days the recipient of such generic usury and grants to the poor.[90]

What did the bishop in the Three Companions' account mean when he said that Francis's money might have been gotten illegally? At first glance, the answer seems evident enough: the bishop meant that Francis had sold his father's goods, and therefore the income belonged to his father and could not be used by Francis for religious purposes. Now it happens that while this dictum indeed reflected standard church teaching, the doctrine of restitution at this time was more complex than it had been earlier. The development of an urban economy had recently generated a great mass of wealth earned in commerce. Much of it—according to the canons—was illegally gained through selling at unjust prices, or through taking interest or usury. This was considered a type of theft. Often the actual owner of these purloined goods could not be determined, commercial transactions being as complex as they are. Some theologians and canonists were in fact discouraging churchmen who came into possession of such uncertain usury from using it for church building. If anything, they favored its distribution to the poor as an alternative. Indeed, in the opinion of Robert of Courçon, a leading theologian of Francis's time, there was one kind of usury that should be given to the poor even in the event that the victim of that usury was known.[91]

Thus, as simple as the bishop's judgment seems to be, it in fact fits into a constellation of disputed legal questions concerning the restitution of theft. At a decisive moment in history, this relatively new campaign against usury influenced the telling of Francis's story. We have already seen that, beginning officially in 1254, after the Three Companions and 2 Celano but before Bonaventure's Life, the Franciscan order had received papal authority to imburse just such uncertain usuries. This would seem to indicate that the order had already been doing so, and had been taken to court for the practice.[92] At the very time when the Companions told their story of the

90. On the ordinary's rights in usury matters, see J. Baldwin, *Masters, Princes, and Merchants: The Social Views of Peter the Chanter and His Circle* (2 vols. Princeton 1970) 1.301; Trexler, "Death and Testament," in *Church and Community* 245–288. For Piccardo, see above, at note 40.

91. This was in cases where borrowers conspired with lenders to pay usury; Robert of Courçon's view is outlined in L. Little, *Religious Poverty and the Profit Economy in Medieval Europe* (Ithaca 1978) 181. On the whole problem see Baldwin, *Masters* 1.68, 108–109, 302–311 (esp. 310); 2.48–49. Baldwin speaks of a "campaign against usury" in the period from the reign of Alexander III through the Lateran Council of 1215. See also his work, "The Medieval Theories of the Just Price. Romanists, Canonists, and Theologians in the Twelfth and Thirteenth Centuries," *Transactions of the American Philosophical Society*, n.s. 49, pt. 4 (1959) 1–80.

92. See above, note 39.

episcopal legal judgment according to which Francis could not rebuild churches with money that might have been badly acquired, this whole question of the restitution of usury was being disputed.

From these few words in the sources about illicitly earned goods also sprang some question about whether Francis himself had sinned in having possession of illegally gained goods. The Three Companions' bishop certainly implied that he had, although Francis himself seemed just as sure that he had the right to pass that money on to others. But was Francis so sure? Another source dwells further on the matter. The so-called Munich Legend, written only a few years after Bonaventure's *vita*, compels us to reconsider the matter: it says that Francis went to the bishop *because he was unsure if he could pass the money further.*

In this account, Francis had sold *his* goods with the intention of applying some of the money to the church, the rest going *in usus pauperum* or for *usus pios*. When Pietro then tried to seize (*extorquere*) the money from him, Francis, despite his intentions, "carefully considered how he could get rid of it, *but licitly.*" He therefore went to the prelate, "and in his presence . . . resigned not only the money but his clothes."[93] There is no indication that Pietro was present. According to this Munich retelling, that is, Francis gave the money to the bishop because he was unsure what to do with it and feared he would be someone's debtor if he chose the wrong recipient! Given the bishop's judgment in the Three Companions that the money might have been badly acquired, we might now imagine that a guilty Francis then stripped himself to repent having stolen the money.

This early story leaves little doubt that contemporary writers recognized that Francis's possession of the money posed serious problems for their evaluation of the prophet of poverty, and that contemporary jurisprudence on questions of badly earned goods was on their minds when they wrote. The Munich Legend even has it on Francis's mind.

The question of Francis's own sin in transacting with his father's money proves to be only the tip of the narrative iceberg of bad money. In all the *vite*, and even more so in his rules, Francis shows a visceral dislike of touching money, and he is pictured as generally avoiding cash, an almost inevitable source of sin. In part this was because those who had gained money illegally were said to pass on the guilt when they passed on the money. At the time of Francis's birth, in fact, the papacy had issued an important decree to just that effect: the inheritors of bad money had to restitute it just

---

93. My italics. "Perpendit, quali modo ab ipsa, dummodo licite, exoneretur, ac coram episcopo civitatis non solum pecuniam sed et vestes . . . resignavit": *AF*, p. 697.

as much as did its original gainers.⁹⁴ It is possible, in short, that Pietro too had been involved in the sin of usury, and that Francis feared inheriting it.

This puts the matter of the money in a different light. In the simplest and probably best reading of the Three Companions, there seems at first no question that the stolen money's proper owner was Pietro; no question of uncertain owners here. But on closer examination it becomes evident that possibly the Three Companions, and doubtless Celano in his second Life, consciously shifted the blame for the badly acquired money to the father. The hereditary taint of badly gained money is part of the story of the renunciation.

Recall that in the Three Companions, the bishop told Francis that the money should not be used for the church fabric, first because it might have been badly acquired, and second, because Pietro was sinning. The text at this point is problematical because the "sin" to which the source seems to allude, Pietro's *furor* or mental derangement, was in contemporary law not a sin at all. On the other hand, contemporaries often said that mental illness was caused by a previous sin, a *culpa precedens*, that God then punished by madness; the classical tag that "mental disturbance is the daughter of avarice" can stand for dozens of medieval moralisms that associated avarice and usury with eventual madness.⁹⁵

I am not ready to impute such a reading to the Three Companions.⁹⁶

---

94. On his revulsion at touching money, see among legions of references *LM*, II, 1. On the canon *Tua* (*Corpus Iuris Canonicum*, X.v. 19. 9), see J. Baldwin, *Masters* 1.305; 2.208, note 65. See further my "Death and Testament," in *Church and Community* 50. On generations damned in this fashion by Antonino Pierozzi, see J. Noonan Jr., *The Scholastic Analysis of Usury* (Cambridge, Mass. 1957) 79. The guilt of descendants was used by the Franciscan missionaries in sixteenth-century Mexico. They took pride that the natives "han dejado otras suertes que sus padres y abuelos tenian usurpadas y con mal titulo: los hijos ya como cristianos se descargan y dejan el patrimonio, aunque esta gente ama tanto las heredades como otros, porque no tienen granjerias"; T. Motolinía O. F. M., *Memoriales e Historia de los Indios de la Nueva España* (Madrid 1970) 238.

95. "Inquietudo mentis, filia avaritiae": the adage is cited by Antonino Pierozzi, *Summa maior* 2 (Paris 1518) c. xcv (bk. 2, tit. 1, ch. xxv). On preceding guilt, see S. Kuttner, *Kanonistische Schuldlehre von Gratian bis auf die Dekretalen Gregors IX* (Vatican City 1935) 84-110, esp. 105 (*mens alienata furore*). A reading of this ambiguous passage to the effect that Francis had wanted to give the money for church repairs so as to absolve his father's sin of anger must be excluded, because the source says the crucifix's orders were Francis's motivation.

96. The Companions (VI, 16) do say that *assumensque pannos diversorum colorum*, Francis sold goods, but they do not say where he got them. Since they then have him leaving the proceeds at S. Damiano, their subsequent statement that Pietro accused Francis of robbing *money* from his house ("quam exspoliata domo asportaverat": VI, 19) is contradictory. But it remains probable that *TS* was saying that Francis had perhaps acquired it badly.

But I am certain, on the other hand, that 2 Celano points his finger away from Francis and toward a usuring merchant father as the actual guilty party. To accomplish this, Celano omitted three salient points from the Three Companions' account he generally adopted. First, Celano omitted Francis's trip to Foligno and the sale of goods, even though he had included it in his first Life and though the Three Companions also told the story.

Second, 2 Celano does not mention the father's sin or his anger as an issue before the bishop. Instead, he has the bishop urge Francis to *resignare* the money to Pietro simply because "it was perhaps badly acquired." But by whom was it badly acquired? Since 2 Celano gives the impression that Francis had fulfilled the command of the crucifix from money he already had, having neither taken any goods from Pietro nor participated in any commercial transaction at Foligno or elsewhere, we can only infer that the bishop was warning Francis that his father might have acquired the money badly in his own commercial transactions.

Celano's third omission seals that implication. For 2 Celano suppressed the Three Companions' story that the bishop cited Francis to appear *ad instantiam*, that is, on the request of his father; as a result, the whole scene in curia reads like one initiated by the bishop *ex officio*. In this second Life, Celano pictures the bishop as a pastor telling Francis not to use the goods for the church fabric because the bishop, in his quality as judge, suspected that Pietro had usured or otherwise obtained the money sinfully. Receiving it back, he and not Francis or the church would then be responsible for its return to a rightful owner.

The Guilt of Francis

Who, then, was guilty? Looking for guidance first to what the biographers say about the particular sum of money in the renunciation drama, we find that the last two Lives, by Celano and Bonaventure, rejected and repressed the whole possibility that Francis was the guilty party. Accepting the Three Companions' dangerous story that Francis had gone to the bishop with the money in hand, 2 Celano nonetheless omitted any potential context in which Francis might have earned such money; indeed, nowhere does this second *vita* of Celano say that Francis, or his father, was a merchant! Bonaventure in turn rejected the whole Three Companions' story, recognizing its inherent danger. He returned to 1 Celano, where an avaricious merchant Pietro "extorted" *Francis's* money from the boy. In this definitive Life, saintly guilt was excised from the beginning.

A close examination of the question of this money has demonstrated that each writer crafted the story so as to make it "fit" his image of the saint's life before the renunciation. Thus, to fully understand the renunciation, it is to that larger biographical context that I must now turn. What type of person was Francis in the *saeculum*? On the answer to that question hinges a second question: what was it that Francis spent the rest of his life repenting?

The foregoing analysis has yielded a striking finding on a central problem of the history and theology of the Franciscan order, one I want to mention before passing to the more interesting matter of Francis's human experience because it forcefully sets the stage for understanding that experience. In 1 Celano and Bonaventure, Francis is a man who had owned property, and he was able to come to the renunciation without guilt precisely because his father had avariciously, and thus improperly, taken the young hero's possessions. In the Three Companions and 2 Celano, Francis is an unemancipated youth who owned no property but only used his father's tainted money. Precisely because Francis had been propertyless, he came to the bishop's curia guilty.

In his dramatic oration in curia reported by the Three Companions, Francis could not say often enough that the clothes, and the money, belonged to Pietro. Five times in that passage he, or the authors, insist upon paternal ownership. I think there can be no doubt that this repetition had a purpose. The Three Companions and 2 Celano were arguing that Francis of Assisi, like Jesus, possessed nothing. This rejected tradition, the very one that does not say that Francis intended to give any of his Foligno money to the poor, defended what would later be called a Spiritualist position in the order, one that insisted on strict poverty.

As a general proposition, it has long been recognized that the Three Companions and 2 Celano leaned toward strictness.[97] But, since one of the central questions in Franciscan historiography has always been Francis's intentions for his order, it is surprising that only what the primary sources say were Francis's utterances after he left the *saeculum* have been the subject of scrutiny on that score. His behavior before then, as constructed by these sources, and especially the tale of the renunciation, has not drawn attention. As far as I can determine, modern scholars have not noted that, obviously glossing questions of poverty, the sources conflict as to what Francis did beforehand.[98]

What is truly fascinating about this abstruse problem of the hero's

---

97. Sabatier reasonably explained Celano's shift in emphasis by the fact that a lax general ruled at the time of his first Life, a strict one at the time of the second: D. Muzzey, *The Spiritual Franciscans* (New York 1907) 68.

98. Failing to note this recently is W. Chr. Van Dick, "La représentation de saint François d'Assise dans les écrits des Spirituels," in *Franciscains d'Oc. Les Spirituels ca. 1280-1324* (Fanjeaux 1975) 203-230.

property or lack of it, however, is the question of Francis's guilt: beyond *imitatio Christi*, what was the object of his lifelong repentance, so often emphasized in the Lives? The biographers present us with clear options: Francis spent his life repenting either for his occupation or for his misspent youth. Over time, the thrust of their *vite* tells us which option to choose: by Bonaventure's Life, it is clearly the simple vices of growing up that have triumphed.

Let me first state, and then demonstrate, the mechanism by which I believe the biographers arrived at this view. Over time, writers converted Francis from a merchant into a knight, and the moral qualities of knighthood were, in this age, equivalent to those of youth.[99] In turn, the biographers employed the virtues and vices of the higher social status of knighthood to separate Francis from his actual occupation as a merchant. Notoriously, the latter way of life caused general disgust among "better" people—and indeed, among legions of merchants.[100] The result was remarkable: the conflict between father Pietro and son Francis became nothing less than a generational conflict between two different social statuses.

The historiographic process is quite impressive. In Celano's first Life (I, 1), Francis is the predictably decadent son of equally bad parents but, rare in a merchant, he is prodigal with his money. Thus, by definition, the repentance that is the driving force of Francis's gifts to churches and to the poor before the renunciation could not have stemmed from guilt for merchant theft or avarice.

The Three Companions partly echo this first characterization. "Although he was a merchant," they say, Francis was a free dispenser of wealth; an early variant of that source compares him to his father in that respect: in his business dealings he was "very different from Pietro, being far more high-spirited and open-handed."[101] A still more insistent theme in the Three Companions is that people regularly mistook Francis for a knight because of his manners *and* his charity: an "indication of his nobility," for

---

99. See Trexler, *Public Life* 387ff. Especially informative on this score is H. Feilzer, *Jugend in der mittelalterlichen Ständegesellschaft* (Vienna 1971). 1 Celano I, 1 is most schematic, saying Francis was vainglorious and proud but, "quia praedives erat, non avarus sed prodigus, non accumulator pecuniae sed substantiae dissipator, cautus negotiator sed vanissimus dispensator." On Francis as knight, see Manselli, *San Francesco* 50–58; and on the high-medieval switch in emphasis from noble and youthful sins (pride and vainglory) to the merchant sin of avarice, see L. Little, "Pride Goes before Avarice: Social Change and the Vices in Latin Christendom," *American Historical Review* 76 (1971) 16–49.

100. On prejudices against merchants, see Baldwin, *Masters* 1.262–269.

101. "Licet erat mercator": *TS*, I, 3. See the translation of the early fourteenth-century Sarnano manuscript in Habig, *St. Francis* 891; also 857, 880.

example, was that he gave his clothes to a poor knight.[102] The logical conclusion of this ennobling process comes then in Celano's second Life, where Francis makes no commercial transactions whatever. Repeating (I, 1–2) the theme of Franciscan nobility from the Three Companions, 2 Celano *does not even mention that either Pietro or Francis was a merchant.*

Determined, as he says, to tell the real story of Francis, Bonaventure does recognize these facts, but in truth his Francis is not really a merchant after all. Other merchants are avaricious (*cupidos*), but Francis puts his trust only in spiritual lucre—and in his *Legenda Minor*, Bonaventure got rid of even that ambiguous conceit.[103] Nobles like Francis were different, Bonaventure wants his reader to believe, and the official biographer adopts the knightly intimations in Francis and the story that Francis himself had always wanted to be a knight and lord. Retelling a story in the Three Companions about Francis's charity to a destitute knight as an indication of Francis's own noble spirit, Bonaventure says that in dressing the knight, Francis "simultaneously fulfilled two duties of piety in one act: he concealed the shame of the noble knight and eased the penury of a poor man."[104]

All the Lives of Francis represented merchants as avaricious but nobles as generous, of course. And like other contemporaries, these writers associated the virtue of liberality not only to the class or status of the nobility but with the age of youth. Thus, by approving a corporative type of charity, practiced by Francis and recommended to future Franciscans, Bonaventure fused the virtues of youth and nobility, of a generation and a status, to contrast this bundle of virtues with the unremitting avarice of merchants.

The result of this ennobling of Francis over time, and of Bonaventure's unwillingness to deny that Francis was, after all, a merchant, is to focus the reader's attention on the sins of youth, rather than on the status of Francis's former occupation. The alternatives were neatly spelled out in a sermon, perhaps wrongly assigned to Bonaventure but certainly written as early as the 1250s. It identified the "society of youth" Francis had formerly belonged to as a "perverse society," and those in it as "associates in sins."

---

102. "Ipse, qui naturaliter erat hilaris et iocundus. . . . Quoddam tamen magnae curialitatis et nobilitatis indicium . . .": *TS*, II, 4, 6.

103. Compare Bonaventure, *LMin, de conversione*, I, to *LM*, I, 1.

104. "Eum . . . vestivit, ut simul in uno geminum impleret pietatis officium, quo et nobilis militis verecundiam tegeret et pauperis hominis penuriam relevaret": *LM* I, 2, and further *LM* I, 3. It is significant that in Bonaventure's view, friars had a duty to clothe the shamed poor of noble standing, even though they were in rags; see my "Honor and the Defense of Urban Elites in the Italian Communes," in Frederic C. Jaher, ed., *The Rich, the Well Born, and the Powerful* (Urbana 1973) 64–78 and G. Ricci, "Naissance du pauvre honteux entre l'histoire des idees et l'histoire sociale," *Annales E.S.C.* 38 (1983) esp. 170.

Francis's former merchant friends, thereagainst, had belonged to a "mundane society"; its sins were not mentioned.[105]

Bonaventure himself dwells on these "sins" of youth. Francis was not only liberal, says Bonaventure, but prodigal. No source can bring itself to say how Francis sinned. No one says that the youthful Francis fornicated, or even that he might have committed the sin of lechery. But our sources do have him engaging in youthful parties and festivities; indeed, he is pictured as the king of the revels. These are peccadillos of lechery, I suppose, but in 2 Celano and Bonaventure they are the sum and substance of what might have been Francis's personal reasons for a subsequent lifetime of repentance.

Of course, the thrust of the biographers is not to say that Francis spent his later life merely repenting his own growing up. Gradually they convert Francis into a peerless youth who, like Jesus a knight of poverty, had the sins of all humanity to redeem. Like most people of the age, the biographers could not take the sins of youth too seriously. Did Francis not intend to be liberal, though he was prodigal, and sociable, though he took part in youthful riot? For a modern audience at least, the pious ruse ends by being unconvincing. Francis certainly did not spend his life in hair shirts and ashes in order to repent his fun-filled rites of passage or the sins of humankind. The Lives seem to obscure, even as they earnest, what Francis must have rued, and then rejoiced in escaping.

We ask again, who was guilty, but this time in the hope of reading between the lines of the historians to find the young man himself. In doing so, one must of course avoid the standard hagiographic practice of projecting saintliness back into the hero's predestined youth. A realistic setting has to be discovered before Francis's own character can be divined.

That realism has been provided by more recent scholars, who now generally accept the Three Companions' version that Francis came to the bishop with the money.[106] On the very eve of the renunciation, he had evidently not yet developed his future taboo against handling money or selling goods.

Nor was Francis a boy who loved to touch lepers. That story too is a retrojection, unfortunately one perpetuated in Raoul Manselli's biography of the saint.[107] As 1 Celano (I, 7) and Julian of Speyer (II, 11–12) demon-

---

105. Found in Bonaventure, *Opera omnia* 9.591. See note 80 above, regarding this source.
106. See e.g., Manselli, *San Francesco* 34ff.
107. But not by Miccoli, "Conversione" 784–785. Manselli's argument that Francis associated with lepers before the renunciation was based on a misunderstanding of Francis's testament, in which he talks of the association and then says, "e poi poco stetti ed uscii dal mondo": Manselli, *San Francesco* 42. The argument is, of course, implausible on its face: few persons

strate, when Francis later recalled that before he left the world he cared for lepers, he referred to the lengthy period after the renunciation and before he donned a habit. By placing the story in the post-renunciation period, these early biographers show that the hardships a humbled Francis faced in that period first made associations with lepers possible. Predictably, the Three Companions (IV, 11-12), followed by 2 Celano (I, 5), advanced the story to before the renunciation, for the obvious purpose of making Francis seem a vessel for divine providence.[108]

And as I have already suggested, Francis's experience before the crucifix of San Damiano is still another case of retrojection from the post- to the pre-renunciation period.[109] When Francis went before the bishop, he was really still very attached to the *saeculum*. Francis would renounce his goods to spite his father, and only *then* discover what he had escaped and had now to repent.

In my view, Francis had been giving goods to the poor in part because he felt that he, and his father, had them unjustly as an inherent byproduct of their occupation as merchants. In renouncing the merchant life, Francis was renouncing not only what he had been doing up to that point— committing sins simply by profiting from his father's usurious and unjust pricing practices—but renouncing as well an inheritance of tainted money whose guilt he might otherwise never escape. The biographers' efforts to transform the hero reveal what the probably tormented, ill, and pious son of a merchant must actually have felt as he assessed the situation: not only sorrow for youthful peccadillos, but relief at repaying his thefts to the poor and joy at fleeing his father's ill-gained goods . . . once that was forced upon him.

The learned biographers of Francis were sensitive to this matter of the money precisely because the just disposition of those badly earned goods whose rightful owner could not be determined was a matter of contemporary dispute, *and* because the Franciscans were claiming that they were poor by definition, and had a right to them. The series of renunciations in the Lives must therefore be seen as commentaries on these central contemporary issues of badly gained goods *and* their transfer from father to son.

Generational tension may be timeless, but its virulence varies accord-

---

in that age would have come near Francis if he had associated with lepers, yet the events surrounding the renunciation find Francis in society and in his home at every turn.

108. Bonaventure, in turn, placed the association with the lepers both before (from *TS*) and after (from 1 Celano) the renunciation: *LM* (I, 6 and II, 6). He also placed Francis at San Damiano both before and after the renunciation.

109. On the retrojection of the miracle of S. Damiano, see also my analysis of the panel by the follower of Guido da Siena, below.

ing to the property institutions of particular epochs. Francis's age had seen the beginnings of a campaign against usury, and the endless declamations against it often indicate no more than that questions of ownership and responsibility for restitution were still legally unfixed. Such uncertainty was bound to affect negatively the relations between fathers and sons, which in turn would affect the way the story of Francis was told.

Celano's first Life and Bonaventure finessed these questions by having Francis shed himself of what he had earned *before* he renounced, so that the renunciation became a simple symbolic rejection of the merchant inheritance. Bonaventure, especially, was not going to put the bishop, the "father of the poor," into the picture.[110] The Three Companions and 2 Celano, however, directly confronted two issues of contemporary concern: that of a father who went to the bishop so determined to get his money back that he risked being found guilty himself of having earned the money illegally, and that of the "sinful" son in the throes of a legal passage to emancipation. Here, Francis's symbolic rejection of inheritance was a spiteful afterthought of the realization that, even though he had sinned in the merchant life, he did not have the right to rebuild churches with those ill-gained goods. We have seen that the Munich Legend of Francis, in modifying the Three Companions' story, wished to leave no doubt as to what was being described: on the one hand charged to rebuild the church but on the other importuned by his father for the return of the money, Francis "carefully considered how he could be rid of it, but licitly."

Ultimately, the conflict in the narratives over whether or not Francis had the money when he renounced his father, and whether the bishop acted the judge or not, rests on contemporary questions of importance to the relations between merchants of different generations. Francis's legal status emerges as important. The question of whether hereditary and earned wealth of those wishing to join the Franciscan order could be given to one's family or had to go to the poor is a part of the earliest tradition. Concern about the definition and proper distribution of stolen goods, including those whose owner was not known, floated out of the accounts. No wonder Bonaventure chose the neat and relatively nonconflictual model he did, for his times required a different Francis, one who was without guilt at the time he renounced because he had owned property. And little wonder that this complex narrative inheritance would fascinate the fathers and sons of a merchant world, and fill them with anxious guilt and fear of each other.

---

110. Indeed, the ordinary's ancient title, "father of the poor," was being challenged by the Franciscans' claim that Francis (and implicitly his successors), held that title: 1 Celano I, 28 and II, 10.

MOTHER PICA REVEALED

In these five accounts, the father matters. *Mater misericordiosa*, Pica released Francis from the chains Pietro had bound him in, and then vanished. These sources never mention her again. These male clerical writers devote all their remaining attention to the bad relations between father and son—to their money problems and callings, and to their separation. In the image they create, Francis passes from one world of men to another, from his father Pietro to the father bishop—or better, so as to honor Bonaventure's determination to keep Francis clear of the bishop and his authority as much as possible, to his predestined men's world of friars.

Suppression of the mother's role is quite in keeping with the tenor of the times. Women's legal rights in many areas, including their right to testify, to inherit, and to control or recoup their dowry, were under siege.[111] This precipitous decline of the public woman was another societal turning-point that influenced the telling of the story: Pica is almost invisible because, historically, women were in the process of losing their *personne morale*.

And yet the difference between the friars' stories and what the notarial documentation led us to expect could not be more striking. From the latter angle it seemed that Francis might have been operating as much or more with his mother's money as with his father's, and that the renunciation had to have involved more substantive matters than the proceeds of one sale of cloth and not a primarily paternal estate that no clerical son could tap without his father's consent. I argued that the drama of renunciation could not be grasped without considering mother Pica and her family situation.

That approach was right. There is much that is important in the accounts we have studied, above all the "man's business" of the character of the money these accounts highlight but disagree on. Obviously, that question of the possible taint of the money sheds light on the nature of Francis's conversion and on the Franciscan order's later conflicts over property use. For all that, our main interest remains who and what Francis renounced, and these five standard sources do not even suggest what our notarial documents make so probable: a role for Pica in the drama. An underground tradition does.

Rome 1475, the third year of the reign of the Franciscan scholar and pope Sixtus IV. Bonaventure, who died in 1274, remains uncanonized,

---

111. There is a large bibliography on the decline of women's rights in this period. For changes in their property rights, see M. Bellomo, *Ricerche*, esp. 52–59, 174–175, 191–192, 200–220, and chs. 1 and 2 of his *La condizione giuridica della donna in Italia: Vicende antiche e moderne* (Turin 1970).

despite his stellar deeds as Franciscan minister general and, in his last year, as cardinal-bishop. Sixtus initiates canonization proceedings that end successfully in 1482.[112] Obviously in connection with Sixtus's initiative, the writings of the epiphanic Bonaventure receive renewed attention, and the most popular of the lot, the life of Bonaventure's and Sixtus' spiritual father St. Francis, is published in an Italian translation.

The first edition appeared in Milan in 1477; it was reprinted there with insignificant changes in 1480. These two are the only fifteenth-century printings of Francis's Life in any language. Both begin by referring to the author merely as *il reverendissimo patre e doctore eximio messer Bonaventura cardinale de la sancta matre ecclesia*. That is, the ancient general was still only a candidate for sainthood.[113]

There can be no doubt that it was Pope Sixtus IV's patronage of Bonaventure's memory that created an audience for such books. These incunables in turn served as sources for Franciscan preachers, who had every interest in promoting a new cult. There being, apparently, no further Italian translations of Bonaventure until the second half of the sixteenth century, the picture of Francis's life and specifically of the renunciation given in these early vernacular imprints was for more than three quarters of a century the only source available to that large readership of saints' lives in translation. The thespians who filled the streets with *sacre rappresentazioni* of the Lives of the saints would, for example, have used these translations, or oral transmissions based on them, as sources for their plays.

And yet, how different might translations be from the Latin accounts they claimed as originals! On reading this influential translation's account of the renunciation, we discover a striking variation from the Latin text, one all the more curious because otherwise the translation is generally faithful to the known Latin text tradition. This variant touches directly on the question of what Francis had renounced.

Recall that the Three Companions and 2 Celano did not explicitly address that question. Instead, they leave the impression that the renunciation was merely the willful act of a spiteful son. 1 Celano and Bonaventure, on the other hand, pictured father and son discussing, before going to the bishop, what Francis was to renounce. But remember too that at precisely this point the generally faithful Bonaventure slightly modified his 1 Celano

---

112. Manselli, "Bonaventura."

113. *Vita del glorioso seraphico padre messer San Francesco compilata per* . . . (Milan: mgr. Antonio Zaroto da Parma, 6 February 1477); *Incomenza la vita del glorioso* . . . (Milan: messer Philippo da Lavognia, 15 January 1480). This translation is preceded by an anonymous Italian legend of the time on the birth and infancy of Francis: see Abate, "Storia e leggenda," 351–352, 365–366.

source and the similar text in Julian of Speyer: whereas they said that Francis went "renouncing in [the bishop's hands] all his rights," Bonaventure's Life says Pietro wanted Francis "to renounce in [the bishop's] hands all *paternal* rights and render everything that he had."

Now we can see that Bonaventure's change was not at all inconsequential: Bonaventure clearly wanted to narrow the inheritance to the father's property! The proof is in the printed Italian translation, which would have none of this narrow construction. Bonaventure says, in the translation, that Pietro sought and found the money at San Damiano:

> And once he had gotten it, he was a bit more at ease. And his fury now gone. and the thirst of his avarice being somewhat slaked by having received the money, the father of St. Francis, well knowing that [Francis] was a son of grace, considered taking him before the bishop of the city to get him to [swear] in the [bishop's] hands *that he refused the inheritance of his mother*, and that he would render to [the father] all those things he had. And Francis was happily ready to do the will of his father. Then he immediately went before the bishop like a person desirous of temporal poverty, and humbly got undressed. And he rendered the clothes to his father, *refusing whatever temporal inheritance of the father and the mother*. Indeed he pulled off his very leg stockings and, throwing them at the feet of the father and the bishop, said: "Take them, father. So from now on I can say: 'Our Father. . . .'"[114]

This remarkable account rings with an authenticity the more telling because in it, the ghost of mother Pica rattles the bones of Bonaventure's story of merely paternal inheritance not once but twice. Let us be sure, however, what the document says, and into which tradition it fits. I begin with the obvious. Assuming for a moment that when Bonaventure wrote he had at his disposal only the biographies I have analyzed, it is clear that he changed

---

114. My italics. "E riceuta che lhebbe, un pocho fo rehumiliato. Et manchato suo furore et la sette de la sua avaricia alquanto cessata per la receuta moneta, si penso il patre de S. Francescho, sapendo bene che lui era figliolo de gratia, de menarlo denanti al vescove ala citta per farli refutare ne le sue mane la heredita de la matre, et egli glie rendesse tutte quelle cose che havea. Et Francescho alegramente fo presto ad fare la voluta del suo patre, dove incontinente andaro davanti al vescove si come persona desiderosa di poverta temporale, et humilmente se spoglia. Et rendi le vestimente al patre, refutandoli ogni heredita temporare de patre e de matre. Etiamdio se trasse le calze de gamba, gittandole denanti al patre et al vescove, dicendo: 'Togli patre, peroche da hora inanti potero dire: "Pater noster. . . .'": 1477: ch. 2; 1480: A-v-verso. As far as I can determine, only one historian has cited the italicized words: F. Attal (Soter), *San Francesco d'Assisi* (Padua 1947) 95–96. He did so only because he was using Italian translations of the Latin texts (although his reference was in Latin, to the "Legenda S. Francisci").

1 Celano and Julian of Speyer either because he wanted to erase intimations in 1 Celano that Pica too might have had wealth—a reading Bonaventure would want to dismiss—or because, while recognizing that she did have wealth, he did not, for a reason soon to be suggested, want that maternal estate to be renounced by Francis. For Bonaventure, Pica did not belong. It was the paternal inheritance that was in question.

The Italian translation begins by following Bonaventure and 1 Celano to the effect that Pietro met with his son and broached an idea. Now 1 Celano's idea was that Francis would renounce everything he had, and so the translation could be considered an elaboration of that source. But Bonaventure's idea, in the authoritative Latin text, was that Francis would reject all his paternal goods, and so the translation stands in direct conflict with that text. First Francis would renounce the *future inheritance* of his mother, and second he would render to his father all the *things*, "cose," of the latter that he *presently* had. The only inheritance mentioned at this stage is the mother's. The denouement insists: Francis returned all his father's clothes to their owner, thus renouncing any inheritance from his father, while also renouncing rights to his mother's estate. Our source does not say that Pietro thereby gained any right over Pica's goods, but only that Francis, apparently through words to that effect, counted himself out of any legal right to their eventual disposition. Words were not necessary to renounce his father's estate, on the other hand: the physical gesture of giving up his concrete evidence of past dependence on his father was equivalent to unconditional severance from the paternal estate.

There is of course an implied internal contradiction in the Italian account: on the one hand Francis and Pietro got together like thinking men and agreed on a course of action before going to the bishop, but on the other hand Francis turned spiteful in the event, even taking off his stockings and throwing them at Pietro's feet. But this inconsistency need not detain us. What matters in this translation is that Pica's presence was felt at the renunciation. Otherwise I accept the Three Companions and 2 Celano's story that Pietro demanded and got his money from and through the bishop and that then Francis spitefully renounced. I note merely that this translation's insistence on Pica's estate is incompatible only with Bonaventure's account: by referring to "all" rights, the other sources might mean to include the mother's estate.[115]

115. In a personal communication, Ignatius Brady wondered if the translator of this text printed in the late fifteenth century did not simply misunderstand his Latin source: the text word *femuralia* or hose might have been read as "feminine" and thus become "mother" in a faulty translation. But such a mistake proves quite implausible. The word is found substantially after the critical passage; see Appendix. The idea is also implausible because reference to the mother

How old then is this account of the renunciation? If it were found only in late fifteenth-century incunables, it might represent a mere whim in an otherwise solid Bonaventuran account of what and who it was that Francis renounced. Further, depending on its age, this Italian text might have implications for our pending examination of the long pictorial tradition of the renunciation.

My review of the written tradition that emphasizes Pica's role confirmed that the variant reading offered by the vernacular text of 1477 and 1480 was not a fleeting anomaly. Let us first consider the later period. The Latin text of Bonaventure began to be printed in the early sixteenth century, and from the start these imprints carry the classic text's reference to paternal goods alone.[116] I have not, in short, yet found a Latin text that parallels the Italian cited above. Nor do the pertinent bibliographical authorities show any edition of the Italian translation in question after the 1480 Milan imprint. No other Italian translation appeared, either. Only in 1557 does a different Italian translation of Bonaventure's *vita* appear, to be re-edited in editions of 1582 and 1616; it faithfully translates the traditional Latin text of the *vita*.[117]

When I looked for the antecedents of the 1477 and 1480 Italian tradition of the renunciation, on the other hand, I found proof that these imprints do in fact rest upon a tradition that long predates movable type. How old that tradition was and in what languages it was preserved is for future scholars to determine. I myself only wanted to be sure, first, that the variant reading was not the work of the anonymous fifteenth-century writer whose legendary account of Francis's infancy precedes the incunables. Second and more important, I wanted to establish that the variant reading reached back to a point in time where its presentation of the renunciation could be derived from pre-Bonaventuran readings and elaborations of the renunciation. For if we exclude the English friar Roger of Wendover, who

---

occurs in two different places in the Italian text. I could find no similar passage in several Latin manuscripts I examined in Rome, and no such variants in the critical editions of Bonaventura's *Legenda*. I would not be surprised, however, if they did exist.

116. A Paris edition of 1507 (*pro Symone vostre*) is followed by a 1508 Pavian edition (Iacobo de Burgho Francho) and then two Florentine editions in 1509 (Giunti; Piero Soderini), etc. I checked the Parisian and Pavian imprints.

117. *Vita et costumi del glorioso santo Francesco composto per S. Bonaventura* (Venice: transl. by a devout friend of Michel Tramezino, 1557); *Vita . . . nuovamente tradotta in lingua volgare . . .* (Venice: Giunti, 1582); *Vita . . . corretta nuovamente e purgata da molti errori* (Venice: Zaltieri, 1616). I also checked a 1512 German translation: *Die Legend des heyligen vatters Francisci. Nach der beschreybung des Engelischen [!] Lerers Bonaventure* (Nuremberg: H. Höltzel, 1512), c. B-ii-v. It faithfully translates the crucial text from the customary Latin. Above the text is a miniature of the renunciation (fig. 28).

seems not to have been read by those in the main tradition, it was Bonaventure who first insisted that only the paternal inheritance had been involved.[118] To establish that our tradition had an independent life well before the incunables would suggest that Bonaventure, as official biographer, had modified 1 Celano specifically to rule out a reading of the event centering on the mother.

I have laid the foundations for this hypothesis by discovering that three modern editions of medieval manuscripts of an Italian translation of Bonaventure's Life all follow the variant reading.[119] This congruence shows that the variant reading was widespread, indeed canonical in the vernacular tradition as far as it can be traced. That is, I have found no evidence of an Italian translation other than that with the variant reading. Among the three editions in question, that of Domenico Manni of 1735 is the most significant for our purposes, thanks to the authority of this skilled diplomatist and the information he gives on his manuscript sources.

Manni used two Tuscan manuscripts for his edition, which as regards the crucial passage are essentially identical to the passage I quoted above. The Florentine manuscript is dated 10 February 1394 by the scribe, who says that he made his copy from a manuscript in the Florentine Franciscan friary of Santa Croce. The second manuscript is not dated; Manni decided that the scribe was Pisan and that the copy was made about mid-fourteenth century.[120]

Without any good reason, scholars have ascribed this translation to the mid-fourteenth-century Dominican Domenico Cavalca or to his cohort, the Augustinian Simone de' Fidati.[121] At the end of the fourteenth century, in any event, the friars of the famous house of Santa Croce owned this variant *vita* of their hero-founder. In it, mother Pica's property was Pietro's first concern, once he recognized that his son was determined to leave the

---

118. For Roger, see above, at note 77. For the anonymous Italian writer, see above, note 113.

119. B. Sorio and A. Racheli, eds., *Vite de' santi padri di Frate Domenico Cavalca, colle vite di alcuni altri santi* (Trieste 1858) 558 for the crucial text, 4–5 for his manuscripts. L. Amoni, ed., *Vita S. Francesco a divo Bonaventura composita. Vita di S. Francesco di Assisi volgarizzata da Fra Domenico Cavalca* (Rome 1880) 30–31 for the crucial text, alongside the classic Latin text. The author does not take note of the variance. D. Manni, ed., *Vite di alcuni santi, scritte nel buon secolo della lingua toscana* 2 (*Delle vite de' santi* 4) (Florence 1735) 160–161 for the crucial text.

120. "Copiata del libro nello armario dello studio del chonvento di frati minori di Firenze": Manni, p. xv.

121. C. Delcorno, "Cavalca, Domenico," in *Dizionario biografico degli Italiani* 22 (Rome 1979) 578. Assuming that the Italian version postdated Bonaventure's Latin text, it is more likely to have been translated by a Franciscan.

saeculum. I think that we shall not be wrong in assuming that by mid-fourteenth century at the latest, when renunciation scenes were being painted repeatedly, Franciscan preachers at Santa Croce were telling their enormous audiences that the mother's property was the prize of the struggle between the bad father and his heroic son. I suspect that further research will push this story back into thirteenth-century Italian or even Latin manuscripts. As I shall show, that story of the mother is convincingly documented in the earliest pictorial tradition.

The recent attention given by scholars to the position of women in late medieval Italy has left little doubt about their importance in public as well as in private life. Whether at Venice or Florence, where such questions have been extensively studied, or at other centers, where work on these problems is less advanced, women are found if not at the center of ritual life, then surely as major property holders, interfamilial mediators, and transmitters of civic culture.[122] It is no longer possible, in short, to accept without question, as matters of fact, men's ideological exclusion of women from descriptions of public life.

As regards the story of Francis, this means that we must ask how the practical-minded laity of Italy *did* understand this story. Was it possible for them to imagine the family without the mother? In the first part of this work, I tried to determine the actual structure of Francis's family. In the second part I studied what the clergy made of the family and its scion, and concluded that the Italian story—that told from the pulpit—was probably different from the Latin one. Clearly, at this point we have only begun to understand what ordinary people made of the story.

I have tried to lay the groundwork for such an understanding by isolating some of the fundamental social facts that shaped the original story and its subsequent transformations. The changing nature of the Franciscan order was, I hope to have shown, of central importance. Because of its peculiar urban and mendicant character, however, changes in that order also closely paralleled movements in society at large. I isolated three such movements. The rise of a commercial economy led men to try to concentrate necessary capital, and that effort caused a long-term attack on and decline of the rights of women. Second, a new campaign against usury or the profits of that

---

122. S. Chojnacki, "Patrician Women in Early Renaissance Venice," *Studies in the Renaissance* 21 (1974) 176–203. C. Klapisch-Zuber, *Women*, and her important review with P. Braunstein, "Florence et Venice: les rituels publics à l'époque de la Renaissance," *Annales E.S.C.* 38 (1983) 1110–1124, esp. 1121. Also P. Labalme's introduction to *Beyond Their Sex: Learned Women of the European Past* (New York 1980). Natalie Zemon Davis has studied Lyon's women in her *Society and Culture in Early Modern France* (Stanford 1975).

commercial economy coincided with Francis's lifetime and that of his biographers. Instigated by the secular clergy but exploited by the mendicants, this campaign created significant social tensions. Among these tensions, thirdly, none was more predictable than that between fathers and sons, for the usury campaign raised the question of what belonged to whom, and whether children could escape the moral and legal "sins" of their fathers. As meager as is our knowledge of the Umbrian ambience in these early centuries, it is clear that there, as in large parts of Europe, dependence, gender, and generations took specific forms as a result of these great social movements.

Thanks to its vast resources and the scholarly attention devoted to it, we can see the products of these Europe-wide tensions most clearly in Florence, where the Italian translation of Bonaventure's *vita* was perhaps done and—just as important—where so many paintings of the renunciation delighted and instructed the laity. For example, I have described the Franciscans as a religious order whose self-definition as mendicant had important implications for the circulation of lay monies. In Florence, we know that the income of the Franciscan friary of Santa Croce became the charge of a municipal official, the "minor syndic," who circulated much of it back into the lay economy.[123] The Florentines, therefore, knew that the discourse about religious poverty was also about civic wealth.

Again, I have described a *giovane* or young man who had apparently not been legally emancipated by his father before he reached his majority of twenty-five years. The Italian jurisprudents' interest in legal emancipation already suggests a widespread fear among fathers of losing their wealth to sons who resented being kept dependent. But if that were not enough evidence, Florentine fathers left a vivid record of generational conflict in their many memoirs (*ricordanze*) and civic chronicles. The pattern of increasing conflict between the generations is clear, so much so that the so-called Last Republic of Florence (1527–1530) from one angle looks like a three-year war between fathers and sons.[124] Still again, the resentment of husbands at wives who poured money into the religious establishments of their sons so that the sons would support them once they were widowed was not limited to Florence, but Florentine merchants talked about it often enough.[125] We can say with confidence that the Florentines, steeped in the art of preserving

123. See above, note 31.
124. On Florentine fathers who said their sons wanted them dead, and on the Last Republic, see Trexler, *Public Life* 369–399 (esp. 389–390), 521ff.
125. See above, note 59.

property in the face of changing legal institutions, would have comprehended the story of Francis and Pietro as a conflict over property.

Second, despite the peninsula-wide attack on women's rights, Italian males in general suspected that women owned the world. Less dramatically: in many areas of the peninsula, women's enormous dowries were the key to male business activity, and the tinder that sparked and meliorated the endless conflicts between grown men.[126] At Florence we can study the facts in detail, and arrive at some startling determinations about the influence of women. By the late fifteenth century, something approaching ten percent of Florentine girls were being forced into nunneries, most of them to enable fathers to finance the marriage of one daughter of the family. Or consider this: the largest item in the consolidated public debt of Florence during the fifteenth century was the state dowry fund, women's money.[127] Was not the conflict over women's wealth the true essence of the story? So must Florentines have heard and seen the story of Francis.

The famous "Florentine marriage pattern" furnishes another angle from which the Florentines could have imagined the story somewhat differently than other Italians. Here in the fifteenth century women married early but men very late and often not at all. Thus, young, often twice- and thrice-married widows crowded the Florentine scene. As first one husband and then another died, endless scrambling ensued for freed-up dowries between old men and young men of different families. On hearing from the pulpit that father Pietro had wanted Francis to renounce his mother's estate, as we have suggested they did, Florentines would have assumed that the mother of the saint had already been widowed.[128]

Unless instructed otherwise, they certainly would have begun by assuming that Francis renounced potential maternal as well as paternal legacies. For that is precisely what boys did in Florence before professing one religious order, at least in the fifteenth and sixteenth centuries. In formal notarial acts, they renounced any inheritance from their fathers *and their*

---

126. See the bibliography in note 122, above.

127. See most recently A. Molho, "L'amministrazione del debito pubblico a Firenze nel quindicesimo secolo," in *I ceti dirigenti nella Toscana del Quattrocento* (Florence 1986) 191-207. For the population of nuns toward the end of the Quattrocento, see my "Le célibat à la fin du Moyen Age: Les religieuses de Florence," *Annales E.S.C.* 27 (1972), esp. 1333-1342. This article somewhat underestimated the percentage of nuns earlier in the century, however; Herlihy and Klapisch-Zuber, *Les toscans* 157-158.

128. Recently on women's wealth and widowhood, C. Klapisch-Zuber, "La femme et le lignage florentin (XIVe-XVIe siècles)," in R. Trexler, ed., *Persons in Groups: Social Behavior as Identity Formation in Medieval and Renaissance Europe* (Binghamton 1985) 141-154.

mothers. In three cases at my disposal involving Benedictine professions in 1457 and 1523, abbots first ordered fathers into their presence for the solemn acts. The boys then began by "renouncing the paternal and maternal inheritance." Next, the fathers on the spot, but soon the mothers as well, "consented to and gave license" for this so-called contract (*patto*). This act having been notarized, the boys then professed as Benedictines.[129]

Admittedly this documentation regarding Benedictines in fifteenth-century Florence does not prove what the penitential Francis did in the thirteenth century, notoriously inflexible though such procedures tended to be. A serious study of early renunciation documents linked to professions remains to be done.[130] But this documentation does convincingly suggest that, *pace* the Latin Bonaventure, fourteenth- and fifteenth-century Florentines had every reason to believe the preacher who told them that Francis renounced his mother's goods as well. Indeed, the words of the notarial renunciations referred to above are all but identical to those of the Italian translation of Bonaventure.

I have sketched the Florentine background not because this city was unique, and certainly not because its urban experience was identical to that of other Italian cities. Rather, we are fortunate to have this knowledge of Florence's social history because it was in that city that so many of the paintings were to be seen and studied. Urban dwellers would, I think, have understood that clerical interests were at stake in the official fashioning of Francis, and the same denizens would have come away from sermons about the hero edified to be sure, but also skeptical about what the preachers said. They would have looked to the paintings, that most popular of media, to

---

129. In the 1457 case it appears that the postulant and his brothers made the contract, which was then approved by the parents: "Martedi a di 8 di marzo 1456 [sf], Filippo, non avendo fatto professione, rinuntio alla redita paterna e materna e in ogni legittima che gli sapartenessi. Facesi con consiglio di dottori per la legge finale di patto. E io Francesco consenti al patto. Fece con lui Giovanbattista per se e in nome di Tomaso e di Girolamo. E fu di patto e cosi si promisse dargli fiorini 25 per uno breviario. Avengha che lui non volessi niente. Funne rogato. . . .

Poi a di 19 daprile 1457, Tomaso e Girolamo ratificarno e io detti licenzia, rogato. . . .

Poi a di 24 di maggio 1457 la Mea consenti e ratifico al patto sopradetto e dette licenzia a tutti, ecc., rogato. . . .": *Archivio di Stato, Firenze, Carte Strozziane* II, xvi-bis, ff. 22r (*ricordanze* of Francesco di Tommaso Giovanni). For the 1523 cases and potential inheritances "o per conto di suo padre o di sua madre," see *Ricordanze di Bartolomeo Masi, calderaio fiorentino, dal 1478 al 1526*, ed. G. O. Corazzini (Florence 1906) 248, 265.

In a 1498 mendicant case kindly furnished me by C. Klapisch-Zuber, where a Strozzi male professed as a Dominican *before* renouncing, the rights passed to the house, which then itself renounce them: *Archivio di Stato, Firenze, Carte Strozziane* IV, 353, f. 6v.

130. See my observations at notes 57 and 69.

confirm their practical sense of what the story of Francis's renunciation involved, just as artists and friars certainly had fashioned the paintings so as to mirror as much as possible the faithful's own experience.

Condensed representations of a reality as complex as the viewers' own, these paintings more than any other medium will tell us how Francis's renunciation was experienced in Italian lay society. I believe that the earliest pictures, fashioned in the pre-canonical period before Bonaventure, actually helped create the story. Working then with a fixed text, the later paintings, even to the end of the fifteenth century, responded to the motor forces of Italian civic experience.

3

The Renunciation According to the Pictures

The pictorial accounts of Francis of Assisi began not long after Tommaso da Celano's first biography of the saint, written in 1228. Berlinghieri painted his famous panel of the miracles of Francis in 1235, but, presumably because the renunciation was not a miracle, did not include it.[131] However, the so-called Master of the Bardi St. Francis, who painted the first true vita of the saint, did paint the renunciation, and his work may in fact be as old as Berlinghieri's. From this time until the popularity of the theme declined in the early sixteenth century, the Renunciation of St. Francis was an almost mandatory scene in pictorial versions of the saint's Life.

Yet there are dangers in focusing attention upon the renunciation to the exclusion of other scenes in the figural vite. After all, some painters were trying to make general statements about Francis. The goal of the present work is not, however, to determine any particular artist's programme overview or intent. Rather, the purpose is to shed light upon a major turning point in the life of Francis and indeed of all humans: the passage from adolescence to adulthood. For the social historian, the benefits of concentrating on that life passage outweigh any neglect of the artist's larger goals that might result. Nevertheless, in what follows I shall analyze pictures of other parts of Francis's life when they facilitate our understanding the social history of the renunciation.

Given this angle of view, what are my goals in studying this corpus of

---

131. See the date on the painting in A. Smart, *The Dawn of Italian Painting, 1250–1400* (Ithaca 1978) pl. 1; further Blume, *Wandmalerei* 15. On the earliest picture of Francis himself, in Subiaco, see G. Ladner, "Das älteste Bild des hl. Franziskus von Assisi," now in his collection *Images and Ideas in the Middle Ages* 1 (Rome 1983) 377–391.

renunciation scenes? One goal is to learn something about artificial- and kin-family relations during those nearly three hundred years. This is practicable because the paintings do not emphasize the legal act of renunciation. Only one late painting in the tradition (fig. 11) seems to show Francis either swearing renunciation of his familial rights *in manibus episcopi* or enacting any of the rites for entering the clergy or taking up penitential life.[132] The paintings are more about emotional ruptures in family relations—rites of passage—than about rituals of clerical contract. We may therefore hypothesize that this series of representations over time documents the changing character of social relations in general, and does not merely record a single early Duecento event in Assisi.

Of five thirteenth- and very early fourteenth-century paintings, two are altarpieces from Tuscany and the other three are frescoes painted in Umbria. After 1300 the scene shifts to Florence, and from then until the sixteenth century that center produced the most Renunciations. This is fortunate, because Florence's social history has been studied far more extensively than that of any other Italian city. To the extent that these pictures document the societies of their painters, we can indeed make the pictures speak about social structures and the emotions they produced.

Yet these paintings do also try to recapture specific historical events of the year 1206, and it is a second goal of the following analysis to isolate the historical imagination of painters trying to seize the moment of Francis's renunciation. Examining these pictures as historical documents is, of course, a daring undertaking, but not a foolhardy one. Let me start with these historical givens, which will control and limit my speculations: the first two paintings are pre-Bonaventuran; one was executed and both were conceptualized before the literary tradition was canonized. Next, bear in mind that painters may be the first to report a story that is only later incorporated by writers. Or, as will be shown here, painters, in addressing their lay audiences, may preserve an event in a realistic setting that clerical authors, in order to make the saint's life seem preordained, hagiographically retroject into an earlier context. Third, three of the crucial early paintings were done in Umbria, where the saint had lived. Last, all the artists relied on some literary authority. Earlier ones knew some, and later artists probably knew all, of the written *vite* of Francis.

---

132. The mid-fourteenth-century fresco at S. Ginesio (Marches) shows Francis, uniquely, turned toward the bishop, but with his hands raised and not in the prelate's: Blume, *Wandmalerei* 63. The standard ecclesiastical renunciation of worldly goods *in manibus* is studied in an unpublished paper of M. Pajes Merriman, "A Case of Royal Rage: Ambrogio Lorenzetti's Siena Fresco of S. Louis of Toulouse." I want to thank Prof. Merriman for the opportunity to read it.

Our study of the early, thirteenth-century paintings in the context of the developing literary tradition on Francis's life will lead to some striking results. I shall argue that the first extant painting was done before the Three Companions' *vita* and the second under that source's influence. More important, these two paintings tell a substantially different story about the events surrounding the renunciation than those done under the influence of Bonaventure's authoritative *vita* of 1263. Painting on the walls of Assisi and Gubbio in the Franciscan fatherland within a few years of the publication of Bonaventure's Life, the next three artists dogmatize. They tell Francis's compatriots and the pilgrims, "This is how it really happened!" Different the representations certainly are from the now-forbidden story! I shall follow this history in the making by closely comparing the early pictures to the written Lives.

The very nature of pictorial representation calls for another level of inquiry. There was much to portray from this man's remarkable life but limited space in which to do so. I shall show how space limitations constrained the artists to combine stories and thus consciously violate the narrative of their sources on the renunciation. It is well known that artists did combine scenes in this way, and yet one recent art historian has said (wrongly) that a certain Renunciation "portrays the moment at which" Francis did something.[133] This is no different from the way medieval preachers taught their audiences "what happened" through pictures. Similarly, an important recent work on saints' Lives cites a *painting* of the renunciation as authority for the authors' narration of the event! In fact, one detail of their narrative which, they say, "everyone knows," is in the paintings but not in the written texts.[134] Artistic conflation of different moments in time into one space creates an erroneously rich understanding of the single event, and evidently scholars too may remember what they see more than what they read.

By deconstructing these paintings, therefore, one can test the fidelity of the texts to the early pictures and then vice versa. We must always keep in mind that the earliest paintings were interacting with a literary tradition still being formed, and that the later paintings all were done at a time when Bonaventure's narrative authority was unquestioned. We can ask how much the artists were constrained by limitations of space to combine events recorded in the texts, and to what extent they rather changed the scene(s)

---

133. E. Baccheschi, in *The Complete Paintings of Giotto* (New York 1966) 91.
134. The authors say that Francis "stripped off his elegant clothes": Weinstein and Bell, *Saints and Society* 49ff. The sources actually lead us to presume he had been in rags for some time. Alas, the authors also misread the written evidence, saying one Ser Bernardone was Francis's father: ibid. 8. On preachers teaching from pictures, see Blume, *Wandmalerei* 113, note 43.

so as to communicate something different to their viewers. Once this is done, we may inquire whether the audience of such painters wanted a "truth" that was predominantly historical in nature, or one that agreed with their own social reality. We already know that the writers had paid attention to their times.

FOUR DUECENTO RENUNCIATIONS

The oldest extant painting of the renunciation is called the Bardi St. Francis because for centuries it has been in that family's chapel in the Franciscan church of Santa Croce in Florence (fig. 1). It is usually dated around mid-thirteenth century. Like 1 Celano and Julian of Speyer, however, this altarpiece does not contain a scene of *the* great pre-renunciation miracle, that of the talking crucifix, nor the Dream of the Lateran. We may therefore assume, I think, that the anonymous Master of the Bardi St. Francis did his work before the appearance of the Three Companions' Life in 1246, the first to mention these episodes. The argument is admittedly *ex silentio*, but it is hard to imagine the crucifix scene of San Damiano being omitted if it had been known, so central did it immediately become to heralding not just Francis's stigmatization, but the hero's world-historical mission. Since the *tavola*'s third picture, which shows Francis designing a habit in the form of a cross to ward off demons, is missing from Julian of Speyer, writing about 1235 (as well as from later writers until Bonaventure), a possible date for this painting is before that year 1235 and after the year 1228 of its source 1 Celano. Arguably, the Bardi St. Francis could even be older than the Berlinghieri miracle painting of the same year 1235.[135]

The Bardi St. Francis *vita* is unique in one respect: it is the only painting in the whole corpus of Franciscan Lives that shows a domestic scene of the saint's family. Before the renunciation, Pica is represented releasing her son from his house arrest, with Pietro di Bernardone standing alone on the margin of the scene. It is the first case of ahistoricity encountered in the pictorial

---

135. This dating would, however, be indefensible if other scenes clearly depended on post-1246 sources. For now, note that one scene of the Bardi St. Francis, the healing of Bartolomeo of Narni, is essentially a quote of the same scene in the Berlinghieri *tavola*. For the traditional date of the former, see L. Marcucci, *I dipinti toscani del secolo XIII* (Rome 1958) 28. The text of 1 Celano I, 9 reads: "Parat sibi ex tunc tunicam crucis imaginem praeferentem, ut in ea propulset omnes daemoniacas phantasias." Thus, as noted by Blume (*Wandmalerei* 15), Celano does not say this design was made in the presence of a prelate, as shown by the painting. Cf. *JS* (III, 15) and *TS* (VIII, 25), who omit the detail of the cruciform. 2 Celano omits the whole incident, known as the mass of St. Matthew. *LM* lifts it from that context (III, 1) and retrojects it to the renunciation (II, 4). Rona Goffen's *Spirituality in Conflict: St. Francis and Giotto's Bardi Chapel* (University Park, 1988) will deal extensively with this altarpiece.

tradition, for we recall that the father was away when Francis's mother released him. Pietro's mood is significant. He seems to beckon his son to him without any sign of the rage the sources attribute to him when he returned and found his son gone. For whatever reason, the artist chose to represent on the margins of the scene a caring, entreating father.

The following scene of the renunciation reinforces this image of domesticity. Mother Pica is again prominent, standing in back of her husband with her hand on his side. As they both look toward Francis, Pietro either beckons to his son not to leave him or he stretches his hands out to get something from the boy. He does not challenge his son. Both parents stand there equally powerless before a son who obviously takes the lead. Francis, standing to the bishop's side, defiantly throws down before his father all his clothing but his underpants.

Francis can defy Pietro because, in the Bardi St. Francis, he is protected by the bishop, who extends his cloak over the young activist. The prelate sits on his *cathedra* with a baldachin over his head. But it is the bishop as judge rather than as pastor who is portrayed here. To leave no doubt on that score, the artist shows both bishop Guido of Assisi and his clerk holding the books on which episcopal judicial decisions are based, books that are omitted where they are not called for, as in the following scene of Francis designing the Franciscan habit. The three central features of this painting are, therefore, domesticity, the bishop as judge in the renunciation, and the immanent nature of both scenes. There is no reference to the supernatural world.

The next oldest representation of the renunciation forms part of a tempera panel attributed to a follower of Guido da Siena (fig. 2). Since this *tavola* includes the talking crucifix and the Dream of the Lateran, it was certainly done after 1246; on stylistic grounds, historians usually date it about 1275 or even as late as the early fourteenth century. Yet we must not be trapped by assuming that every painting derives all its details from a literary source. In fact, the most important thing about this tavola is that it preserves information on the earliest history of the Franciscan cult that no extant writer reported. This surprising fact must be documented before I examine the renunciation scene itself, which was certainly painted under the influence of the pre-Bonaventuran tradition of the Three Companions and 2 Celano.

The evidence is simplicity itself: the story of the miracle of San Damiano is painted after the renunciation, which introduces the *vita*, and not before. Further, in the San Damiano scene Francis is pictured with the crucifix not as a layman but in Franciscan habit, leaving no room to entertain the idea that this sequence was an accident of the artist or of his Franciscan patrons. Thus, an event that all the writers who mention it place before the renunciation is pictured here after it. To make the significance of this panel still clearer, let me prefigure my analysis of subsequent paintings: the renunciation will introduce the first two painted *vite* that follow the *vita* of Bonaventure—that in the lower church of Assisi and that at Gubbio—just as it does this one. Yet in this Sienese altarpiece, the miracle of St. Damian is a scene separate from the renunciation. That will not happen again until the third pictorial vita following the publication of Bonaventure's Life.

To interpret this remarkable variant, let us begin with the commonsensical assumption of any student of medieval society that this painting does show the order in which things actually happened. Recall that neither Tommaso da Celano nor Julian of Speyer knew anything about such a San Damiano vision before the conversion. More important, visions registered with the medieval public after a person converted, not before, to form thenceforth the basis of his or her support. The probable scenario is as follows. Francis probably converted without anyone but a small group of relatives and friends knowing or caring. It is possible that shortly afterwards, however, a rumor spread that a crucifix at San Damiano had talked to Francis, one of the many penitents who roamed the streets and suburbs of this typical medieval town. This would have attracted city-wide attention and, perhaps, Francis's first nondestitute followers. Whether the sequence in this painting has a literary foundation or not, it reflects the laity's common experience of holiness.

And yet, since the first two authors and the Master of the Bardi St. Francis also do not record the miracle of the talking crucifix as having occurred either after or before Francis's conversion, it appears that the story did not circulate until well after Francis's death, indeed after 1235, the date of Julian of Speyer's Life, the last written source to know nothing of the incident. Probably the Three Companions incorporated the story from a recent oral tradition, but the possibility must also be considered that later writers simply concocted it out of something that is mentioned later in the first Life of Celano and of Julian of Speyer, ones that know nothing of a miracle at San Damiano. The story of Francis's stigmata is of course such a tale, and the talking-crucifix miracle at San Damiano is indeed a form of prefiguration of the stigmata.

I see a strong possibility that something between these two extremes took place. First, all the biographers place Francis at San Damiano not only before but also after the renunciation: Francis rebuilt the church then that he had earlier tried to aid monetarily. Indeed, all the writers dwell on his later activity there. Celano's first Life is particularly noteworthy in this respect, since his account contains the most striking imbalance in the attention given San Damiano before and after the renunciation. This was with good reason: in reality, it was afterward, while Francis was at San Damiano and at the nearby Porziuncola, that he became known and began to attract followers.[136]

This actual and literary context, I would speculate, is the ultimate seedbed of the Sienese painter's representing the miracle of San Damiano *after* the renunciation: a story was now circulating that the San Damiano crucifix had talked to Francis after his renunciation, and the long 1 Celano and Julian of Speyer accounts of Francis at that site furnished the inspiration for the hagiographers. One of two things happened. First, it is possible that the Three Companions themselves transformed an oral tradition without mediation, so that the miracle took place before the saint's renunciation; in this reading, there was no literary model. A second and more likely scenario emerges, however, once we take into account the fact that the Three Companions retrojected to a point before the renunciation other stories that Celano placed later, notably the tale of the lepers whom Francis cared for and fearlessly kissed on the mouth.

Since neither Celano's first Life nor Julian of Speyer knows anything about a miracle at San Damiano, therefore, I would hypothesize that the post-renunciation miracle comes from a lost text of the Three Companions, or that the Three Companions moved the story forward from an earlier, today unknown, literary account that had described the miracle as occurring after the renunciation. This account, or an earlier inextant painting with that account, would have been the painter's source at Siena. Whatever the truth of the matter may be, however, this painting shows that some late thirteenth-century Franciscans, at one with the everyday experience of their flocks, understood the miraculous life of the young Francis to have begun *after* his renunciation.

Let us turn now from the Siena painting's San Damiano panel to its picture of the renunciation (fig. 2) and compare it to its predecessor. The mood is different from that of the Bardi St. Francis: here there is no dramatic movement, either on the lay left or on the ecclesiastical right; the two sides are linked by Francis's gown hanging limply from Pietro's left arm. The bishop sits in his chair of justice without books, protecting Francis by having

136. 1 Celano I, 7-8; *JS*, II, 13-14; *TS*, VII, 21-24; VIII, 25; 2 Celano I, 8; *LM*, II, 7-8. On how medieval people discovered holiness, see my *Public Life*, intro. For the date of the Sienese painting, see J. Stubblebine, *Guido da Siena* (Princeton 1964) 107ff. Note in the Renunciation the vestige of an inscription on the church pediment.

him stand between his legs as well as by placing his red cloak around the youth. Francis, for his part, draws attention to the bishop, by almost dreamily opening up his left hand in the prelate's direction.

Despite the poor condition of the painting, the scene of the laity on the left definitely reveals two distinct rows of figures. The three taller men in the back row cannot be certainly identified; perhaps they represent the "youth" who mocked Francis long before the renunciation. The front row is slightly clearer. Francis's father stands closest to the saint, with Pica to his right and rear, and then a young girl in blue, perhaps the matron's servant. The destruction of Pietro's face prevents any assessment of his emotions, but the stance of his body suggests that they were contained. For, as in the Bardi St. Francis, here too the father's right hand is opened out toward his son. Since Francis's right hand is also opened toward the bishop, the effect is that Pietro refers the viewer to the prelate rather than expressing his own anger or avarice. The artist draws all attention to a fait accompli: Francis has become a son of the church.

This happens despite the marked emphasis the artist gives mother Pica. She is taller than her husband and, while all the other spectators look at Francis and the bishop, she turns away from her son and toward the girl behind her; her facial expression, unfortunately, is no longer discernible. Indeed it may be that the prelate and his convert are themselves looking at Pica, for they are not gazing toward Pietro or any other person. The net effect of this damaged picture, therefore, is to make the perhaps mourning Pica the most prominent figure on the left side of the painting. It is as if the artist, not wanting to represent the scene of Francis released from his chains, still sought to evoke its maternal sentiment.

While these two early paintings established one tradition that would remain almost invariable, they adopted two other themes that would end with them. The former is the left-right organization of the secular and ecclesiastical worlds, with Francis mediating between them. Francis's relative intensity and his actions are of course important, and we must treat them as such. But Francis was a vessel for changing social discourses in these paintings, and our attention will more insistently be drawn to the world Francis entered and the world he left in these three centuries of the theme in pictures.

The abortive themes are thus quite as significant. The first of these is the prominent position of the mother, represented now in all three of the paintings we have viewed. In the Bardi St. Francis she is shown as the main personage in the only scene where the written tradition gave her that role, that of releasing her son from chains; that event would not be represented in later paintings. Pica is then present in both Renunciations we have examined, even though the written tradition never suggests she was present. She even dominates the other laity in the latter painting. Alas, she will all but disappear from future paintings of the subject.

The second abortive theme is the bishop's prominence and character: as judge *in cathedra*, he is the authoritative figure in these early paintings. Thus, while the moods Francis casts over these two panels are sharply distinct—the former showing him defiant and the latter immobile—both paintings project one message. Francis is leaving a world of domestic and parental, even feminine, affections; he moves to a male world, but one that is peculiarly anerotic, legal, and structured.

As in the Bardi St. Francis, there is also no supernatural world represented in this Sienese Renunciation; such immanence will disappear from the following paintings, but then return in the fifteenth century. These are not paintings of the Bonaventuran legend, where every Franciscan act is an allegory of heavenly predestination and meaning. Rather, these two earliest paintings radiate the domesticity and episcopal justice important to the less miraculous first Life of Celano, and especially to the Life of the Three Companions.

We dwell in closing on the mother, so important in these paintings and yet the most inconsequential of figures in the Latin written tradition. Why this disparity? I think the answer is that in this more popular medium of figurative art, messages had to be more believable. Pica is represented so prominently because she was a *personne morale* whose money was at stake, just as she is found to be the object of Pietro's concern in the Italian translation of Bonaventure. In her figured presence in the paintings, contemporaries would have seen represented, I think, her wealth in dowry and property, the objects over which men fought in real life—as little as they might have wanted to talk about it.[137] Thus we can see a continuous record of that always present, if uncomfortable, force of the woman in the Franciscan story from these two paintings to the Italian translation of Bonaventure, documented from about 1350 onward.

Any doubt about the pre-Bonaventuran date or inspiration of the previous paintings will be erased by our study of the next two surviving works, frescoes that show a new world built around an authoritative text. The first is on the north nave wall of the lower church of San Francesco in Assisi (fig. 3), and is conventionally attributed to one Master of St. Francis. The other is in the upper story of the right apse of the church of San Francesco in

---

137. On this theme, see the text above, at note 114. The presence of persons in paintings was often taken to document their actual presence as a legal personality; see e.g. Blume, *Wandmalerei* 113, note 43.

Gubbio (fig. 6), and presently has no attribution. Historians agree that both were painted in the second half of the thirteenth century, and on stylistic grounds the Gubbio scene has a fairly secure *terminus ante* between 1280 and 1285.[138]

A mere glance at the two frescoes and at the Dream of Innocent that follows both of them suffices to show that one painting inspired the other, though they are certainly by different artists.[139] The same glance also assures the viewer that one and probably both of these paintings were direct sources for the famous representation of the renunciation in the upper church of Assisi (fig. 7), usually dated around 1300. Except that the churchmen are on the left in the lower church of Assisi but in their more decorous place on the right at Gubbio, the spatial organization and the placement of figures is redundant, and very different from the older paintings we have already examined. The painter of the renunciation in the upper church adopted the Gubbio placement, and it remained canonical thereafter. Because of this adoption, and for another reason having to do with decorum to which I will return, I think that the Gubbio painting postdates by a very few years that in the lower church of Assisi.[140]

Turning back now to the Renunciation in the lower church of Assisi, we find that it, together with the Dream of Innocent, occupies a once-unbroken wall surface that since about 1320 has opened into the Montefiore Chapel of St. Martin painted by Simone Martini.[141] That rupture half destroyed the Renunciation, leaving the clerical left side intact but on the right a mere half figure of Pietro di Bernardone, who holds a red cape presumably retrieved from the largely nude Francis.

Among those figures that have survived, two attract our notice. The first in importance is Francis, whose seemingly stilted, archaic representation is so striking as to almost succeed in diverting our attention from what the young hero is doing. He is falling. His right leg seems to collapse and his left buckles, as his hands extend up toward heaven. Francis is clearly not

138. Blume, *Wandmalerei* 32, 153-154; Belting, *Oberkirche* 88, 169-171; J. Schultze, "Zur Kunst des 'Franziskusmeister'," *Wallraf-Richartz Jahrbuch* 25 (1963) 121-122, 131.

139. Belting, *Oberkirche* 88, 169-171; Blume, *Wandmalerei* 32-33.

140. Blume also dates the Gubbio frescoes after those in the Assisi lower church, but only because of a narrow iconographic reading involving the representation of a seraph; ibid. 13, 32; his reading is also that of J. Cannon, "Dating the Frescoes by the Maestro di S. Francesco at Assisi," *Burlington Magazine* 124 (1982) 65-69.

141. E. Borsook, *The Mural Painters of Tuscany* (Oxford 1980) plates p. 23, has a sound *terminus ante quem* of 1317 for the opening of the wall; cf. Boskovits, "Celebrazioni" 214. I cannot find a literary source for the fragmentary caption of uncertain date beneath the renunciation scene (". . . vestibus exutus . . . evangelica iussa[!] . . ."); cf. G. Ruf, *Das Grab des heiligen Franziskus. Die Fresken der Unterkirche von Assisi* (Assisi 1981) 51.

recoiling from his father or reaching up to God as to his new father. Evidently, he has been struck or suddenly possessed by God, much as if he were in the midst of an attack of epilepsy, the sacred disease.[142] He is in ecstasy, and I shall isolate the historical event that is involved when I turn to the Gubbio fresco. Supporting this enraptured figure is the bishop, his throne nowhere in sight, who holds the cloak covering Francis with his right hand. Behind the bishop are five clerks. We will see these citizens of the city of God in many subsequent pictures, just as in most later paintings a group of laymen on the opposite side will stand for the city of Man.

Yet these clerks are not of equal importance. The one directly behind the bishop is particularly prominent here, as he will be in several later paintings. He turns slightly more toward the viewer than do the others. Both in his dress—he wears an ornate cape quite different from the others' clerical garb—and in painterly relief he stands out, so much so as to momentarily distract attention from the saint's unabashed ecstasy. We have chanced upon a person who will preserve his prominence in later paintings even when artists themselves were unsure why their predecessors had conceded that prominence to him.[143]. The literary tradition knows no such figure. Who then can he be?

The Gubbio fresco (figs. 4-6) supplies a surprising answer: the figure

142. Not noting Francis's sharp withdrawal, Blume imagines the young man telling God that he, and no longer Pietro di Bernardone, is his father: *Wandmalerei* 121. Compare this figure to the exorcised figures in the last scene of Berlinghieri's panel: Smart, *Dawn* pl. 12. A figure similar to Francis is the exorcised woman in the *Très riches heures* of the Duke of Berry, reproduced in I. Lewis, *Ecstatic Religion* (Baltimore 1971) pl. 8a. Celano extensively describes the falling disease (*caducus morbus*), which "quidam malignum fuisse diabolum opinentur": 1 Celano I, 25, also 26. The same disease, usually called hysteria in women, led Francis at one point to determine "utrum foret daemonium, an deceptio muliebris"; Celano's Treatise on Francis's Miracles, in *AF*, p. 319 (paragraph 156; see further 154, 156, 195). Bonaventure described a similar condition where a certain friar was "quandoque totus extensus et rigidus." It was so horrible "ut magis esse vexatio daemonis quam naturalis infirmitas a pluribus firmaretur"; *LM*, XII, 11, further 10. On this "sacred disease" and the occasional difficulties of distinguishing it from ecstasy, see O. Temkin, *The Falling Disease* (Baltimore 1971) 86-92, 118-134; D. Walker, *Unclean Spirits* (Philadelphia 1981), pp. 10-17. 89. On the distinctions between different ecstasies, see R. Javelet and T. Szabo, "Extase," *Dictionnaire de Spiritualité* 4 pt. 2 (Paris 1961), cols. 2116-2126, and col. 2178 for information on and denial of a relation of ecstasy to epilepsy, as in M. Laski, *Ecstasy. A Study of Some Secular and Religious Experiences* (Bloomington, 1961), 254-255.

143. He is particularly marked in Trecento paintings in the upper church, in Giotto's Bardi Chapel Renunciation, and in Taddeo Gaddi's quatrefoil representation. See further below and figs. 7, 8, 15. In our present painting, the figure is at the center of an almost complete half-circle. He points with his right hand toward the Francis action, his left palm being on his chest. Since the bishop's miter is not facing the action, that prelate may be looking at the figure in question, but the destruction prevents one from being sure.

may be none other than Bonaventure of Bagnoregio! Author of the Life of the saint rendered definitive in 1266, he may be pictured in the lower church of Assisi and at Gubbio introducing the viewers to Francis's Life in this first scene, in effect saying to them: "Welcome! *This* is the way it happened." The Gubbio fresco is particularly persuasive on this score because that figure, though not isolated from the narrative action, remains absolutely central to the viewer. As visitors to San Francesco walk up the aisle, they find this man at its terminus. He it is who welcomes viewers to the drama (fig. 4).

As one comes closer, the man's prominence is still more accentuated (fig. 5). Blond and tonsured, wearing a chin beard like other figures in the painting, "Bonaventure" is dressed much the same as that figure was at Assisi. He raises his right hand to greet the devotee coming up the aisle. At each side stands a tonsured young man, looking not at the drama of Francis but at this master; the one on our right is actually leaning forward so as to hear him. Behind this figure and to our right, two more clerks peer toward "Bonaventure." This person is not just another clerk. To be sure, there are solid reasons, which will be reviewed, for doubting it is Bonaventure. But those who remain unpersuaded by this identification should explain to whom else so many eyes would be turned.

This bevy of persons builds a powerful if disconcerting visual unity separate from the figures of Francis and his father. Bonaventure and the bishop provide the bridge. Having greeted us with the one hand, the Franciscan general and author delicately directs us with his other hand toward the saintly action, and he himself is actually in the process of turning his head to watch. "Don't pay attention to me," a humble author seems to say; "the real story is over there." Yet the bishop of Assisi is not so sure, since he is turning his head back toward Bonaventure, as if to say, "Are we doing it right?"[144]

So striking is this competing formal field on the right side of the painting, and so unmistakable are the links between that field and Francis, that in the absence in the written tradition of an alternate figure who might fit this eminence to whom so many eyes are turned, one is forced to suggest Bonaventure.[145] This formal face, at Gubbio not devoid of all individuality,

144. Compare my reading of the meaning of Bonaventure's hand motions to F. Garnier, *Le language de l'image au moyen âge: Signification et symbolique* (Paris 1982), esp. 105 fig. D. On what else Bonaventure may be saying at Gubbio, see the following note.

145. The figure is probably meant also to give the "Dominus det vobis pacem," the powerful miracle-working greeting revealed to Francis. Once spelled out in his testament, the greeting thereafter was a distinguishing mark of all Franciscans: 1 Celano I, 10; *TS*, VIII, 26; *LM*,

may belong to none other than the author himself. Before proceeding further, one objection to this notion may be put to rest. It was not unusual before or after this time to represent an author in the same visual field as his story. As we shall see, Bonaventure himself was so represented.[146]

Bonaventure's presence in these two paintings would also make good sense in the historical context. Franciscans were violently debating the life of Francis at just this time, and at every turn, new tales were materializing. Had he really been without property? Had he not used it? What was the truth about the stigmata, about his testament, and so forth? Indeed, the heavy-handed order by Bonaventure and the general chapter of 1266 that all other writings on the saint be destroyed first incited the battle between the Spirituals and Conventuals.

What more fitting than to set the record of Francis's life straight in the Umbrian fatherland, and especially in the very burial church of the hero, the pilgrim's goal? The representation of Bonaventure as master of ceremonies would certainly have been intended to have a calming because authoritative effect on viewers, caught in the middle of the vicious disputes wracking the order.

The identification of this central figure as Bonaventure is certainly not without serious, perhaps disabling problems. First of all, he is not represented with the conventional book, as Bonaventure the author is doubtless shown in a Trecento painting by Taddeo Gaddi (fig. 16). A second problem concerns the figure's clothes. In the Gaddi painting Bonaventure is shown as one would expect: he is a Franciscan bishop, a prelacy to which he was appointed in 1273 before being made a cardinal almost on the eve of his death in 1274. Neither in the lower church of Assisi nor at Gubbio,

---

III, 2; Perugian *Legenda,* in Habig, *St. Francis* 1043. *TS* says that before Francis was born, a precursor went through Assisi crying out a similar greeting. But this figure cannot be the one in question in the painting: the precursor was apparently a layman, and the story is not mentioned elsewhere; cf., Abate, "Legenda" 256, further 248. Blume suggests that the figure in question is the person the bishop ordered to get something to cover Francis with, and he notes that that detail first appears in Bonaventure: *Wandmalerei* 23. But here and in the lower church of Assisi this figure is the center of attention; he is much too prominent for that minor role. Besides, the Bonaventuran text (" . . . praecipiens suis, ut aliquid sibi darent ad membra corporis contegenda. Oblatus est autem ei mantellus pauper et vilis cuiusdam agricolae servientis episcopi": *LM,* II, 4) in fact does not refer to a particular person. Finally, one might speculate about the figure being the first protector of Francis and the Franciscans, cardinal Ugolino. I had no success developing that notion.

146. See Gaddi's Tree of Life, described below. For Byzantine book illuminations showing authors pointing up toward their sacred scenes, see A. Grabar, *Byzantine Painting, History and Critical Study* (Geneva 1953) 163.

however, is there any clear sign of the episcopal dignity, and indeed nothing I can discover that surely identifies him as a Franciscan. An examination of the next Renunciation will suggest that its painter may have understood the earlier figures as Bonaventure. Why would he have thought that to be the case? Possible solutions run as follows. First, Bonaventure may be represented as the Parisian *doctore eximio*. Second, he may be wearing a cardinal's gown. Alternately, the pictures may have been painted before Bonaventure was mitered.[147]

Difficult as determining this man's identifying marks may be, there is no doubt that he is a center of attention in both this painting and the one at Assisi: a welcoming host and the viewers' master of ceremonies through the devotional liturgy of Francis's way of the cross.[148] And the tale told is doubtless Bonaventuran. Once allowance is made for the artistic conflation of different events, the renunciation that is represented at Assisi and Gubbio unmistakably bears his mark. That significant fact strengthens my identification of this personage.

Furthermore, that fact makes the now-forbidden legend of the Three Companions the certain source of the Sienese *tavola* we have studied. To the point: now in the frescoes, the bishop's chair and book are gone. The prelate, standing down on the street among mortals, is no longer a judge. Second, the mother is gone. On the surface, this story is now exclusively about men and their money, and not at all about feminine domesticity. Finally, the worldly Francis and the immanent universe of the previous paintings are gone. Francis is now in ecstasy, enacting Bonaventure's portrayal of Francis as a vessel of God rather than as a person reluctantly disengaging from the world. In short, all the characteristics I identified as Bonaventuran in the literary tradition and as conflicting with the tradition of the Three Companions and 2 Celano have now been transferred to the visual narrative. The presence of these characteristics leaves no doubt that both works bear the impress of the official historiographer, vary though they may in details.[149] The historical context, indeed, precludes our being

---

147. On the doctor, see above at note 113. Representations of living lay patrons were common; Enrico Scrovegni, for example, was alive when he was represented in the Arena Chapel of Padua. Live ecclesiastical officials were commonly painted, e.g. giving or receiving books, towns, etc.: J. Beckwith, *Early Medieval Art* (New York 1964) figs. 49, 80, 100. For a mid-thirteenth-century book painting of Parisian doctors, see the frontis plate in Baldwin, *Masters* 1. A fourteenth-century painting of university figures is in J. Le Goff, *Genio del Medio Evo* (Milan 1959) 133.

148. The renunciation, at least in the lower church of Assisi, introduces the *vita*, and on the opposite wall begin the corollary scenes from the Passion of Christ.

149. Blume thought Celano inspired the frescoes of the lower church, Bonaventure those of Gubbio: *Wandmalerei* 32-33. G. Ruf had it right: *Grab* 59-62, and 50 and 192 note 31.

surprised. After all, Bonaventure of Bagnoregio, minister general since 1257, was in charge of the order when the frescoes were put on the walls of the mother church of Assisi.

First of all, the Gubbio painting makes Bonaventure's theme of the two cities explicit, by placing that of God and that of Man behind and above the two groups and thus reflecting Bonaventure's explicit use of allegory. In the city of man there are at least five figures. Two young men talk together about the event, while in front of them stands Pietro, a stately chin-bearded figure in red cloth (like the Pietro in the Assisi fresco) who has already retrieved the clothes Francis had removed. He shows no sign of agitation whatever, as he did not in Bonaventure's account of the renunciation, and rather points toward Francis or Bonaventure as the proper center of attention. To Pietro's left another man points up to heaven, that is, to where Francis himself is looking.

Ultimately, it is the enraptured Francis himself who must be said to command the painting because, on close examination, his tongue seems to hang out as if he is deranged! If we now recall the figure of Francis in the lower church of Assisi, who recoils as if struck by God, we know that the Gubbio apoplectic or possessed Francis is simply a sign for the same phenomenon. In the former painting, Francis seems about to fall down. Here Francis stands erect but his protruding tongue signals the same ecstasy. Surely not by the same painter who worked in the lower church of Assisi, this Gubbio painting on the other hand furnished the painters in the upper church at Assisi the basic form of their renouncing Francis. As we shall see, the latter simply closed Francis's mouth. This greater decorum is a second reason to believe that the Gubbio painting postdates that in the lower church of Assisi.[150]

Yet search though we may, the written accounts of the renunciation itself say nothing about ecstasy. Bonaventure does say that Francis stripped off even his underwear because he was inebriated in spirit in his wondrous fervor (*ex admirando fervore spiritu ebrius*: II, 4), and that passage is in-

---

150. The suspicion proves excessive that a fault on the paint surface creates at Gubbio a mere illusion of a tongue. Let us leave aside the odds that a fault shaped like a tongue would occur at just that point, and discount my observation that the color distribution in the area makes that fault improbable. By following the curvature of the lower face one may be quite sure that Francis had his mouth wide open. Francis's ecstasy in the paintings of the renunciation has not previously been recognized: see e.g. C. Cahier, *Caractéristiques des saints dans l'art populaire* (Paris 1867), 402. Like the falling disease, the rigidity of apoplexy produced symptoms comparable to those given for ecstasy, and like epilepsy, apoplexy was also said at times to be accompanied by loss of facial and tongue control. See the literature cited above, note 142. One should not, to be sure, exclude the possibility that Francis was being represented with the gift of tongues (1 Cor. 14.2).

deed suggestive. But the canonical formula for describing ecstasy—as being outside oneself—is not there. One must ask, then, to which rapture these two paintings refer? A study of the sources leaves little doubt as to the answer: Francis is represented in the ecstasy he experienced when the crucifix talked to him at San Damiano, well before the renunciation.

From its first appearance in the Three Companions, this miracle of the talking crucifix was a central proof of Francis's saintliness while he was still in the *saeculum*. But at both Assisi and Gubbio, the renunciation continues to open and introduce the *vite* just as it had the previous paintings of Francis's Life. The miracle of San Damiano was not yet the separate, preceding scene it would soon become. Thus I suggest that these artists sought to bring the earlier San Damiano experience into this introductory scene of the renunciation. Later artists would not understand this motivation, and would represent separately both the renunciation of an ecstatic Francis *and* the miracle at San Damiano.

Now, it is important to recognize that only Bonaventure said Francis achieved ecstasy at San Damiano. Previous writers had not dared ascribe that state to him. The Three Companions (V, 13) did say that Francis was *tremens ac stupens* after the crucifix spoke, and Celano in his second Life (I, 6) added that Francis "became almost deranged" (*quasi alienus a sensu*) in the event. But it is Bonaventure alone (II, 1) who completed the ecstatic formula the others had not dared: Francis went out of himself (*mentis alienatur excessu*) and had to return to himself before he could continue.[151]

The Bonaventuran version of Francis's San Damiano experience once revealed as the source of these rapturous representations, the Gubbio and Assisi churches' placement of the scene of the renunciation— opposite Innocent III's dream of the renovated church—makes narrative and architectural sense. Recall that it was Bonaventure who first insisted that the San Damiano crucifix had actually been ordering Francis to renovate the universal church, and not really the humble San Damiano. In the figure of the ecstatic Francis we have thus a record of San Damiano on the left, while on

---

151. "Tremefactus Franciscus, cum esset in ecclesia solus, stupet ad tam mirandae vocis auditum, cordeque percipiens divini virtutem eloquii, mentis alienatur excessu. In se tandem reversus . . .": *LM*, II, 1. The stuporous representation thus corresponds to the condition described in the paintings, except that in both 2 Celano (I, 6) and Bonaventure (loc. cit.) Francis is said to have been prostrate when the crucifix talked. Presumably, an account of a saint in stupor on the ground did not lend itself to decorous artistic or heroic representation. Bonaventure considered Francis the perfect ecstatic: Javelet and Szabo, "Extase" col. 2120. E. Underhill describes Francis in ecstasy using 2 Celano's account of S. Damiano cited above: Celano says that Francis came out of S. Damiano a different man than he went in, but he recommends silence rather than daring to call the episode an ecstasy: *Mysticism* (New York 1961) 180-181.

the right is represented the papal dream that someone would soon begin renovating, figured in Francis holding up or rebuilding the universal church/S. Damiano. Most interesting, both paintings of the set, certainly at Gubbio and probably at Assisi before the Montefiore chapel was installed, have a common source of divine light coming through the window separating them.[152]

In the previous pages I have paid close attention to these two Umbrian paintings because of their inherent interest and because formally they represent such a departure from the two earlier paintings. But it is their social distance from the earlier ones that ultimately matters. Here we confront a change from immanence to transcendentalism, from domesticity to severe patriarchy, and from the church as judge to the church as the sexlessly pure alter ego of lay male society.

How does one explain such a profound change? The elements of some partial answers have already been presented, beginning with artistic considerations. By deciding to incorporate the event at San Damiano into the renunciation, the artists in Umbria perforce introduced transcendentalism into the tradition and abandoned the immanentism they might otherwise have retained if they had done the San Damiano scene separately. Such an approach is more convincing than to raise the specter of different Tuscan and Umbrian regional styles. For the formal structure, at least, of the Umbrian paintings in fact soon conquered Tuscany.[153]

Second, it is certainly true that developments in the literary sources contributed to this stark change in representations of the renunciation. Given Bonaventure's determination in his vita to eliminate the bishop-as-judge, for example, it was not to be expected that the bishop *in cathedra* could survive on the walls of Franciscan churches: that in itself goes a long way toward explaining the Umbrian adoption of more or less equally balanced and complementary groups of laity and clergy.

But the exclusion of women in the Gubbio painting and in most of the

---

152. See fig. 5. It is probably because outside light was being used that these paintings have no signs of divine intervention above them; that theme first appears in the upper church of Assisi, and recurs in Paolo da Venezia and then in Gaddi, whereafter Francis no longer looks toward heaven. Note that at Gubbio, Francis faces away from the window. The artist seems to have chosen a proper left-right, lay-clerical organization as more crucial than the light source; inversely, I would hypothesize that the improper spatial organization in the lower church of Assisi was chosen because of a window to the picture's right.

153. Historians sooner distinguish between distinct Florentine and Sienese qualities in the Duecento than between Tuscan and Umbrian styles; Umbrian art of the time is usually viewed as the product of Roman (e.g., Cavallini, Torriti) and Florentine (Cimabue) influences; see e.g., Smart, *Dawn* 9–16; Chastel, *Italian Art* 88–89.

subsequent tradition, and the resultant patriarchal cast of this and most of the later paintings, is not easily explained by literary or artistic imperatives. One must look elsewhere. While it is true that none of the literary sources mentions Pica's presence at the renunciation, it is also true that both of the earlier paintings—the first of which, the Bardi St. Francis, was certainly known to the painters of the lower church of Assisi and Gubbio—had made her a prominent figure in their Renunciations. And the evidence of the subsequent paintings will show that artists repeatedly copied their predecessors and that they did not hesitate to incorporate themes that are not in any written Life. The fact that Bonaventure in his Life said that Francis renounced only the paternal inheritance would not, therefore, explain why not only Pica, but almost all women, disappear from the Gubbio painting and the subsequent tradition.

In truth, the very fact that women, and especially Pica, are absent merely calls attention to them, perhaps especially for societies whose males were so dependent on women for their fortunes. The crucial role of wives in mediating the tensions between family fortunes is clear from recent work on Venice, while students of Florence even now are preparing an edition of the dowry archives, so central are these investments to an understanding of the distribution of wealth in that society.[154] It is obvious that men did not like to talk about this crucial role. For example, David Herlihy has shown how Leon Battista Alberti wrote *Della famiglia* as if women were marginal to the family at a time when they were at the center of society's attention.[155] Evidently, we must view at least some of the innovations in the paintings as documenting profound social changes of the time. No single change is more soundly documented than the continuing decline of women's legal rights in the late Middle Ages.[156] I think that women now largely disappeared from the Renunciations because men wanted to see them disappear from the public world of contracts and finances.

THE RENUNCIATION IN THE FOURTEENTH CENTURY

The creation of a Renunciation that is a patriarchal exchange between the clergy and the mature males, or that shows an exchange between different generations of men, was the achievement of the second pair of paintings we have studied. Another central element in the Francis story, and one

---

154. A recent article by A. Molho is cited above, note 127. Concerning male dependence on dowries, see the bibliography in notes 52 and 122 above. See also the text at notes 126-127.
155. D. Herlihy, "Growing Old in the Quattrocento," in P. Stearns, ed., *Old Age in Preindustrial Society* (New York 1982) 104-118.
156. See above, at note 111.

that was to have a long life, had not appeared yet—because, I would suggest, the times did not yet make the theme acceptable. That was the appearance of an angry father Pietro who turned violent against his own son. This powerful new motif, which is *foreign to the literary tradition of the renunciation*, is first encountered in the fresco of the renunciation in the upper church of Assisi, done around 1300 (fig. 7). Some thirty years later, Giotto drove this theme to a magnificent pitch in his stunning fresco in the Bardi Chapel of the Franciscan church of Santa Croce in Florence (fig. 8).[157]

The theme of Francis's anger with his father had dominated the first Renunciation we studied, that of the Bardi St. Francis where the saint threw his clothes on the ground before Pietro. That motif never appears again. The rage of the *saeculum* with the saint, on the other hand, makes its first appearance in the upper Assisi painting, in the figures of children. There on the left side they introduce the theme of ridicule into the visual tradition, calmly holding the stones that then, on both sides of the Giotto fresco, they actually hurl at the saint.

These children unmistakably incorporate the story of Francis's initial return from San Damiano to his home, when he was mocked in the streets. The first extraneous story brought into the representation of the renunciation was the miracle at San Damiano. This is the second. The ridicule happened after the crucifix talked, and was the immediate occasion for Francis's imprisonment at home. Yet the story appears to have been importantly modified. In the literary tradition, either citizens or young men (that is, the profane *saeculum*) hurled those stones, and indeed, young men of this time did engage in formal stone fights in the street. But the literary sources never say that children threw the stones. Here in the painting, the story conforms to "decency," and children (*fanciulli* or *pueri*) are blamed. The emphasis thus shifted away from peer conflicts to generational ones and, once children were involved, women could be blamed for their excesses. And so a mother or nurse figure creeps into the left corner of the Giotto painting, trying to restrain the babes.[158]

---

157. Recent datings of these two paintings and positions on their disputed authors and relations are offered by A. Smart, *The Assisi Problem and the Art of Giotto. A Study of the Legend of St. Francis in the Upper Church of S. Francesco, Assisi* (Oxford 1971); Belting, *Oberkirche* 222-242; Smart, *Dawn* 16, 29-30, 59; B. Cole, *Giotto and Florentine Painting, 1280-1375* (New York 1976), pp. 96-108, 146-160; J. Stubblebine, *Assisi and the Rise of Vernacular Art* (New York 1985) 16-41, 64-79. On the extent of Pietro's anger in *TS*, see my text, after note 78.

158. The restraining figure on the left is a woman, that on the right a tonsured clerk. For the *pugna saxorum* of the youth, and over and against that, the children's custom of decimating corpses, see my *Public Life* 579 (stone fights) and 582 (judges and popular justice). Cf. note 61 above for the *concives* and *iuvenes* who least of all in Assisi would want their ages shown engaging in such "childish" behavior.

Moving now from these edges toward the angry father and Francis at the center, let us first examine the group of men who escort the bishop on the right side, and then continue to the larger group on Pietro's left. Besides the solemn clerks accompanying the bishop, there is the significant "Bonaventure" figure of the earlier Umbrian frescoes. In the later Giotto painting, he has become a stout and perhaps untonsured eminence in red, still overseeing a performance of which he remains the choreographer, as the bishop's gaze back at him shows. In the earlier painting at Assisi, the thinner figure on the right surely invites identification as Bonaventure himself, since the bishop looks directly to this clerk, who points as if he is directing the scene, for reassurance.

Recall the comparable figures our artist would have had as models. At Gubbio (figs. 4–6), the figure welcomes and directs the audience to the renunciation, while downstairs at Assisi (fig. 3), the same figure, there dressed in a ceremonial cope over a red undergarment, performs much the same functions. The artist upstairs understood, for he seems to have painted a Franciscan, if one without the usual corded belt, as the choreographer. This figure seems purposely to lift his sleeveless scarlet or red outer dress so that the viewer will take note of the stylish mendicant brown habit beneath. Perhaps unconsciously in later paintings but quite consciously here, artists in copying their predecessors may have perpetuated the presence of Bonaventure.

Who is this personage wearing either scholarly or cardinalate red[159] over his perhaps hoodless habit, in this most influential cycle in Franciscan art, if not Bonaventure? The identification of the figure as Bonaventure in the earlier frescoes downstairs and at Gubbio was based on their ceremonial and prelatial posture and dress—especially since those two frescoes introduce their respective cycles. Yet in the poor state of these earlier works it is hard to find much indication the figure was a Franciscan. The same ceremonialism and prelatial character encourages a "Bonaventuran" identification here in the upper church of Assisi, but in this case the figure could be a Franciscan; and it cannot be excluded that a later artist of the renunciation, at San Ginesio in the Marches (fig. 11), also painted Franciscans or Franciscan postulants in the same space. Thus this painting in the upper church of Assisi makes it plausible to say not only that Bonaventure was there from the lower church of Assisi onward, but that some of the millions of late-medieval pilgrims who viewed the definitive vita in the upper church recognized Bonaventure directing the show in the renunciation.

---

159. Scarlet was adapted by the cardinalate in mid-thirteenth century and, it is said, by Parisian masters thereafter: H. Rashdall, *The Universities of Europe in the Middle Ages* 3 (Oxford 1936) 390–391.

Turning now to the retinue of Pietro on the other side of this and the Giotto paintings, I can make some suggestions about its relation to the story by dividing the lay group in two. From the Gubbio fresco on, a group of usually older men surrounds Pietro; beginning in the upper church, these men restrain him. Perhaps they are the "neighbors and friends" Pietro consulted before he first challenged Francis; perhaps, as the official-looking dress of some of the figures suggests, they represent the government of Assisi, which Pietro consulted in the now-forbidden tradition of the Three Companions. Clearly these men were intended to represent, however uncanonically, those who restrained Pietro: we recall that having heard the racket his son's mockers were making when Francis returned from San Damiano, Pietro, in Bonaventure's words (II, 2), "threw compassion to the winds" and "immediately rushed after [Francis], determined to crush him, not to protect him."

Behind this group of men there is another, generally younger set of men. Beginning at Gubbio, continuing here in the Assisi upper church, and in some later paintings, these fashionably dressed young blonds so lack empathy for Pietro's troubled state that, as in the upper church of Assisi, they do not look at him or at Francis, but rather converse among themselves. While the fine figure immediately behind Pietro in the Gubbio fresco (fig. 6) is completely alone, in the moment that children are introduced into the tradition in the upper church of Assisi, this group of youth stands behind the children, as in Giotto's and Gozzoli's Renunciations (figs. 7, 19).

I suggest that these figures represent the *concives* or *iuvenes* who ridiculed the saint on his initial return from San Damiano. The reader will recall that the figures in back of the family in the Renunciation by the follower of Guido da Siena (fig. 2) also may represent Francis's cohorts ridiculing him, and a later painting in the cycle (fig. 19) will clearly show an older reveller ridiculing him. The fresco of the upper church may also hint at this reading. Immediately above the children who hold their aprons full of rocks stands a young man who, along with others, looks away from the action. Forming a unit with the children, he too holds something, a large, uncertain object that extends well down his gown. It is not a merchant's bag; I tentatively suggest that it may represent the bag of a wind instrument.[160]

There may therefore be three generations of Franciscan enemies executing popular justice: children, cohorts, and father. Since there can be little

160. See however the Bardi St. Francis and Giotto's renunciations (figs. 1, 8) where a spot respectively on Pietro's and on an associate's side has been destroyed. This curious dual destruction in the same chapel (since the late sixteenth century) makes one initially suspect an intent to destroy symbols of merchandizing rather than of revelry. On usury as shown in another Giotto painting, see U. Schlegel, "On the Picture Program of the Arena Chapel," in J. Stubblebine, ed., *Giotto and the Arena Chapel Frescoes* (New York 1969) 85.

doubt that the children in the upper church of Assisi and thereafter represent the insults visited on Francis when he first returned from San Damiano, and quite as little doubt that Pietro in the same paintings is shown in that same setting, one may surely return to the Gubbio fresco (fig. 6) and find that very moment represented in the solitary fine young man standing alone on the left. For in that painting there are no children, and Pietro is neither angry nor restrained.

In my view, the youth in festive garb at Gubbio represents this mockery. The painter in the Assisi upper church, who saw the now-destroyed secular figures in the lower church and perhaps too the related scene at Gubbio, introduced the noncanonical figures of children to bring out the theme of insult, and associated to them, in muted form, the insults of the *iuvenes* in the figure over them.

From these close studies of single figures, we have emerged with a better understanding of the whole tradition. First, the theme of social as distinct from paternal mockery or insult is present in all but the early Bardi St. Francis Renunciation. Second, the non-canonical children were introduced to make the representation of insult more "decent" by downplaying peer conflict. Third, starting with the lower church of Assisi, three or even four quite distinct historical moments are shown in a single scene.

First, in the figure of the ecstatic Francis, the founding miracle of San Damiano's talking crucifix is represented. This is true even when, as in the upper church, Francis's prayer before that crucifix is separately represented.[161] For in this Renunciation as well, the hand that reaches down to Francis is probably not just a sign for godfather,[162] but a sign of the very Crucified, who had already reached down to Francis in the San Damiano scene of the Sienese altarpiece. A second historical moment folded into the Renunciations is the mocking of Francis when he first returned from San Damiano, openly by the children and vestigially by the youth; it is on the left side here in the upper church of Assisi, and in several subsequent paintings. Third, the angry Pietro who first appears in the upper church reflects that moment when a humiliated Pietro rushed into the street and continued the beating the citizens had started. This war of the generations is shown to be kept under control by the judiciousness of the good burghers of Assisi. The bishop, and the same father holding the discarded clothes, anchor the fourth and last scene in this scenario, the renunciation of St. Francis.

We have come, finally, to the powerfully angry confrontation of Pietro

---

161. The scene of the renunciation is preceded by paintings of Francis honored in the Assisi piazza, Francis giving his cloak to a poor man, Francis's dream of arms, and the prayer at S. Damiano.
162. As assumed by Baccheschi; *Complete Paintings* 91.

and his ecstatic son, a confrontation that is foreign both to the literary tradition of the renunciation and to its first known representations in the artistic tradition. At Assisi (fig. 7), the father has already retrieved Francis's clothes, and he steps toward the young man with the intention of striking him. He betrays sternness more than anger in his face, however, and the young man with long blond hair merely restrains him gently.

At Florence, Giotto brilliantly heightened this tension (fig. 8). Now Pietro shows true anger in his face, but apoplexy in the instant of behavior in which the artist has caught him. The father at one and the same moment rises up with the clothes he has retrieved *and* lunges toward his son. Just as remarkable, the men in his retinue both help him up *and* restrain the hurt and vulnerable man from his furious attack.[163] This is a moment of genius in the iconographic tradition of the renunciation.

In the preceding analysis, I have shown where in the literary tradition the artists found their story that the father was angry and even attacked his son. I cannot insist too often that the renunciation was not the source. It is little short of amazing that the father begins to be shown in renunciation scenes as angry just when the *vita* of Bonaventure becomes canonical—a biography that portrays Pietro at the renunciation as a model of composure, for the very good reason that, according to Bonaventure, Pietro was the one who engineered the renunciation. Yet the more the Bonaventuran *legenda* took hold, the more the noncanonical figure of the angry father became canonical in the paintings.

Yet it would be ridiculous on several scores to explain this curious phenomenon merely by determining that the figural Renunciations are conflations of different events. That does not really explain why these artists violated the literary canon and introduced paternal anger and violence into the bishop's palace and Francis's renunciation and why that violent image would prove so tenacious in the coming centuries. The artists knew that viewers would take away from these Renunciations, as the essence of that event, a picture of angry father confronting ecstatic son. But that image is unfounded, and justified least of all in the official Bonaventuran tradition. So powerful do the pictures prove, however, that some serious modern writers have retained precisely this false image of events.[164]

---

163. One must inspect the actual painting to see that Pietro's thigh is rising up; it is not clear in photographs. Note however that with his left hand Pietro holds his clothes as if getting up, while with his right he seems to grasp the hem of his associate's gown in doing so.

164. The artists may, in fact, have been representing two forms of mental disturbance in conscious juxtaposition, for all the sources say that both Pietro and Francis at different times were thought to be insane. Still more significantly, contemporaries like Bonaventure classified *furor*, the condition ascribed to father Pietro before he got his money, as one form of the ecstatic condition Bonaventure ascribed to Francis (*mentis alienatur excessu*), as in the term *mens*

Obviously, these paintings are not simply transferrals of written stories to the visual field but vehicles of social commentary. They represented to lay audiences social relations that had to be comprehended in contemporary terms in order to be affective. The story of the renunciation of property had now become, and would remain, a chosen vehicle for the representation of relations between fathers and sons in Italian society. Similarly, the theme of the Marriage of Joseph and Mary would become, again on a Giottesque inspiration, the preferred theme for representing the relations between young bachelors and old men who married young girls. The important question is then, why are fathers now shown first angry and then trying to beat their sons?

As Christiane Klapisch-Zuber has argued in her studies of the theme of the Marriage of Joseph and Mary,[165] so I would argue for our theme of the renunciation: the growing violence of the father toward the son in these pictures is emblematic of a real social conflict between men, fueled by the problem of women's money. Just as did Bonaventure, so will the painters replace Francis the sinning youth with Francis the ecstatic. Father Pietro will remain "furious" as he was before he retrieved Francis's money—as he does in Bonaventure's account—but he no more than his companions will be represented as avaricious. Not one money-bag, symbol of that vice, soils the panels.[166]

Thus, the whole question of tainted money must be read behind rather than in the paintings, which are determined to mask as generational antagonisms the social foundations of that conflict. Most "decently," women will long remain absent from the paintings. Yet the Italian translation of Bonaventure shows women are really vividly present, and in my view are known to be so by the lay audiences of this sacred scene.

The audiences for these Renunciations would remain largely Florentine, although in the years around and after the Giotto fresco at Santa Croce foreign artists tried their hand at the theme and emphasized other elements. In a window at Königsfelden in Switzerland (fig. 9) dated between 1325 and 1330 Pietro, restrained by his companions, tries to attack his son and to prevent him from approaching the bishop. Working about 1360, Paolo da Venezia shows much the same reading of the story (fig. 10), for he has Pietro, perhaps restrained by Pica, actually trying to remove the bishop's

---

alienata furore: Kuttner, *Kanonistische Schuldlehre* 95, and index, "Geisteskrankheit." Incidentally, note from the previous description that the forbidden *TS* does have an angry Pietro stand up at the renunciation after Francis stripped himself. But even this father does not attack the boy.

165. "Zacharias, or the Ousted Father: Nuptial Rites in Tuscany between Giotto and the Council of Trent," and "The 'Mattinata' in Medieval Italy," in *Women* 178-212 and 261-282 respectively.

166. See above, note 160. Note however the round object on top of the clothes in fig. 20.

cloak from Francis—in other words, attempting to stop Francis from joining the clergy.[167]

It is worth drawing particular attention to this theme, for the notion that Pietro resisted his son's entering the clergy is found nowhere in the written tradition. According to the 1 Celano and Bonaventure accounts, Pietro himself encouraged his son to renounce his property rights before the bishop, while in the Three Companions and 2 Celano *vite* it was the father who brought Francis before the prelate, if not for purposes of having him renounce.

From the beginning of the painted Lives, however, there is some note of paternal reticence about Francis's choice. I pointed out that in both the Bardi St. Francis and the Sienese altarpiece (figs. 1, 2), Pietro may be reaching out to beckon his son—away from the bishop. Here now in these two foreign representations, the father's desire to keep Francis from the clerical estate is manifest. It is an interesting reflection of what different cultures saw in the struggle.

But the theme of keeping Francis from the clergy is out of the Florentine mainstream, where violence inexorably increases as women continue to be excluded. We resume our survey. The renunciation scene in the *vita* by the Master of the Franciscan Temperas, of about 1340 (fig. 14), found on an altarpiece in Ottana, Sardinia, is one of the most violent. There a group of young men swings away and back from the church entrance; it takes them all to keep Pietro from breaking through and attacking his son. The father is so menacing that even the bishop raises his arm and hand to keep Pietro away.[168]

At about the same time, Taddeo Gaddi followed Giotto's lead by bringing violent children into the fray. In this quatrefoil on a reliquary *armadio* (fig. 15), the last known Tuscan Renunciation of the Trecento, the children,

---

167. See respectively E. Maurer, *Das Kloster Königsfelden* (*Die Kunstdenkmäler des Kantons Aargau* 3) (Basel 1954) 76; M. Muraro, *Paolo da Venezia* (University Park 1970) 127-128. For the sake of completeness, I include among my illustrations of the renunciation (1) A badly damaged fresco at S. Fortunato, Todi (fig. 12), which is a direct quote from the upper church of Assisi: Blume, *Wandmalerei* 66ff and (2) a badly damaged mid-fourteenth century fresco in the church of S. Fermo Maggiore, Verona (fig. 13), of interest mainly because of its emphasis on Francis entering the (open) church, i.e. joining the clergy; see G. Kaftal, *Iconography of the Saints in the Painting of North east Italy* (Florence 1978) col. 331. I do not include a badly damaged painting of the Venetian Zanino di Pietro (fl. 1407). It is said by Kaftal to be a Renunciation of Francis: loc. cit. 329-332. But the reproduction by B. Berenson (*Italian Pictures of the Renaissance: Venetian School* 1 [London, n.d.] pl. 95) lacks any indication of Francis's nakedness. More probably, the picture, housed in the museum of Rieti, shows the story of Francis clothing the knight.

168. The painter was Tuscan; see the dating in F. Bologna, *I Pittori alla Corte Angioina di Napoli* (Rome 1969), pl. VI (24[29]).

96 CHAPTER 3

who actually throw rocks, are brought into the foreground of the painting.[169] Gaddi's small panel is also the last in the whole tradition to show Francis looking toward heaven. After engendering more violent representations in Assisi itself, the renunciation will emerge powerfully in the early fifteenth century to portray henceforth a purely immanent drama between mortal men.

Before continuing the survey of the theme, let me note that Gaddi has also copied from Giotto the "Bonaventure figure." He is that obese man looking on from behind the bishop and the latter's crosier-bearer. On comparing this figure to Gaddi's figure of Bonaventure as Franciscan bishop in his *Arbor Vitae*, painted in the refectory of Santa Croce (fig. 16) after 1350, one sees that the physical traits are quite dissimilar. It thus seems clear that by mid-fourteenth century, artists had forgotten the original significance of the "Bonaventure figure" in the Renunciations, highlight though they still might the figure itself.

Gaddi's *Arbor Vitae* holds our attention for one further moment. Far from being merely an archaic representation of the Tree of Life, as Donati has branded it,[170] the crucifixion scene in this work is certainly intended to evoke Francis's experience at San Damiano. I showed earlier that at Gubbio, the renunciation scene is conflated with Francis's ecstasy at San Damiano, and at Gubbio, Bonaventure points to that ecstasy. In Gaddi's work as well, Bonaventure, again in the same space as the active Francis, watches Francis with pen in hand and thus evokes the San Damiano ecstasy that is conflated with Christ's crucifixion. Indeed, Bonaventure made the link between the San Damiano and Calvary events explicit in his work *Lignum Vitae*, which is the basis for Gaddi's painting.[171]

In this way, crucifixion paintings showing Francis at the foot of the cross became part of the record of Francis's youth because they evoke the miracle of San Damiano. At San Ginesio in the Marches the parallelism is openly invoked, for there a crucifixion featuring Francis hugging the cross was painted directly below a scene of the renunciation (fig. 11).[172]

From the image of Gaddi until the early fifteenth century, no Florentine Renunciations exist. Elsewhere, however, the violence of the father continued to mount, and by about 1380, pilgrims to Assisi could see an almost

---

169. See A. Ladis, *Taddeo Gaddi: Critical Appraisal and Catalogue Raisonné* (Columbia, Mo. 1982) 114–120.
170. P. Donati, *Taddeo Gaddi* (Florence 1966) 29, 39.
171. I. Brady points to the spiritual presence of Francis in the *Lignum Vitae* in his preface to E. Cousins, ed. and transl., *Bonaventure: The Soul's Journey into God, The Tree of Life, The Life of St. Francis* (New York 1978), pp. xiii–xiv.
172. Cf. Blume, *Wandmalerei*, pls. 152 and 153, and see p. 64 for the layout.

filicidal image of Pietro. This was painted not in any neutral or ambiguous setting, but rather in the very suburban church where Francis had heard the crucifix and in disgust thrown the money onto a windowsill, whence Pietro retrieved it. Until brought to scholarly attention recently by James Stubblebine, the frescoes in this small, dark church of San Damiano had been relatively neglected.[173] Although they do not include a Renunciation, these paintings are important to our theme.

The two works refer to events said to have taken place at San Damiano. On the south wall, Francis prays before a semblance of the famous crucifix (fig. 17). Farther to the west, past the windowsill where Francis is said to have left the money, a terrified priest shies away from an onrushing father Pietro, who holds the clothes he has recouped from his son. Commanding the inside right west wall of the tiny church, a vicious Pietro lunges forward with a truncheon raised to smash his son—in full view of the altar crucifix (fig. 18)![174] How rare it is to find such a violent painting so command a church! It works almost like a giant cartoon to overpower the visitor.

THE RENUNCIATION IN THE RENAISSANCE

Soon, this memorable type of attacking father made his appearance in Florence. Sometime in the early Quattrocento, in a gallery lunette of the first cloister of Santa Croce, alongside, but separate from, a scene of the renunciation, a painter drew Pietro beating his son (fig. 19).[175] The latter scene represents Francis's public humiliation when he returned for the first time from San Damiano. Among the shadowy figures, one can make out on the left two women, one of whom restrains a stone-throwing boy. Between this boy and Francis there seems to stand a young man of the same height as Francis who, with his laurel crown and perhaps a large horn on his right, seems an explicit representation of the fine youth we first identified at

173. J. Stubblebine, *Assisi* 68-69.
174. I share R. Van Marle's view on the dating: *The Development of the Italian Schools of Painting* 5 (The Hague 1925) 65. As noted by Stubblebine, that of 1305-1315 offered by the Assisian historian L. Bracaloni ("Assisi medioevale. Studio storico-topografico," *Archivum Franciscanum Historicum* 7 [1914], 16) is too early; Stubblebine, *Assisi* 69. I am grateful to the since-deceased Stubblebine for visiting S. Damiano and sharing his pictures with me. Blume, *Wandmalerei*, does not mention the church or its crucial frescoes.
175. The neighboring lunette contains scenes that may refer to the conversion of fra Bernardo da Quintavalle. These frescoes are now preserved at the Florentine Villa Corsini by the Tuscan *Soprintendenza alle Gallerie*, and are next to impossible to examine. So I am especially grateful to Dieter Blume for sending me a photocopy of the latter lunette fresco. The Gabinetto Fotografico numbers its photographs of the two frescoes consecutively: 124121 and 124122.

98   CHAPTER 3

Gubbio. To the right stands Francis, who is being pummelled with a switch by Pietro. Behind the father stand three persons, two of them males who seem to be discussing the matter. In the equally badly damaged Renunciation farther to the right, four males can be discerned. They are divided into two groups, the first group standing behind Pietro in discussion and the second group including Pietro and a man restraining him. The part of the fresco with Francis and the clergy has unfortunately been destroyed.

The two scenes at Santa Croce are interesting on two scores. First, they confirm my "festive" and "insult" readings of the left sides of the Gubbio and Assisi frescoes: here the different historical moments are separated where elsewhere they were combined. The artist has lifted the punishing father, the rock-throwing child restrained by a woman, and the festive youth out of the traditional renunciation scene and placed them in their proper element, the return from San Damiano. It is the only fresco of this event I have found, but it shows that contemporaries clearly understood the meaning of these representations in the standard Renunciations. Second, the figure of the second woman, who raises her hands in horror at what is happening, is particularly interesting when we recall that precisely in Santa Croce was deposited a manuscript of the Italian translation of Bonaventure, containing the passage insisting on the importance of the mother's estate. It may be that this is Pica, making a fleeting re-entry into the tradition of the Lives.

By the early fifteenth century, then, Florentine audiences could see alongside a scene of the renunciation one in which father beat son with an instrument chosen for the purpose. This motif of Pietro beating Francis with a truncheon or switch would appear in later Florentine book illuminations (fig. 24),[176] but it does not seem to have been continued in monumental art. Instead, artists later in the Quattrocento kept the old tradition of telescoping different moments into powerful single spaces, and they would soon adopt the belt, Francis's own belt, as the instrument with which the father beat his son.

First, however, the tradition had to transcend the unpredictable and here deliberately archaic Sassetta, who between 1437 and 1444 painted a Renunciation within a polyptych at Sansepolcro (fig. 20). It is a vision that returned to the Duecento for its inspiration. Once again, the bishop sits in his chair of judgment with Francis between his legs. Francis's clothes lie on the ground at Pietro's feet rather than being retrieved by him. As in the Duecento and from now on, the scene is immanent: Francis with crossed

---

176. I shall return to the presence of Pica in both illuminations. My thanks to Vicki Porter for photographs.

arms looks at the clothes and not at heaven. Yet despite these features that hark back to the Duecento, the paternal violence, unknown to that earlier time, is powerfully rendered, almost dizzying. Moreover, the genders of the combatants are different now. Earlier I spoke of a patriarchal society in which Francis moved from carnal to sexless fathers. But here not only the virginal Francis but all the clerical figures are so dainty that I sense an almost sexual flavor of war between the genders.[177] Perhaps as in some other non-Florentine paintings already referred to, Pietro here wants to retrieve his son from this nest of "women" rather than to beat him up. Be that as it may, this painting needs no stone-throwing children to bespeak violence. Pietro's veritable lunge at this virginal, Donatellesque "David" is barely restrained by the father's two male friends.

The classical spatial organization of the renunciation, which had remained the same since the frescoes of Gubbio and the lower church of Assisi, ended decorously in the lifeless fresco of the renunciation by Benozzo Gozzoli, done in the apse of the Franciscan church of Montefalco in 1452 (fig. 21). The caption for this painting is the classic Bonaventuran text, and thus makes specific reference to Francis's renunciation of only the paternal goods. Now the children have retreated to the left-hand corner. The laymen are lifeless, and even the man assigned to restrain the unusually young Pietro barely touches him.[178] The group on the right is quite as listless, and Francis himself has been turned into a terrestrial blond iconette surrounded by the bishop's shiny brocade cloak. Pietro, though about to shout, has a face devoid of emotion. The one element of this painting that retains our interest is that the father holds Francis's own belt, with which he tries to attack the boy.

An old and evidently tired spatial organization, a young man who has become a common earthly icon, male retinues that appear mere puppets for upscale bourgeois capi: this is a pictorial scheme that seems to have nothing more to tell us about tensions between generations in the Renunciations. And yet the story still had life in it. About midway through the fifteenth century, Francesco Squarcione did a Life of Francis in the lunettes of the outside walls of San Francesco Grande in Padua. So badly damaged today that only an outline survives (fig. 22), Squarcione's Renunciation broke radically

---

177. The androgynous quality of the figures is not, to be sure, unusual in the Sassetta corpus. For the date, see J. Pope-Hennessy, *Sassetta* (London 1939) 96-97.

178. Note that the imposing "Bonaventure figure" is definitely a cathedral canon. R. Levi-Pisetzky (*Storia del costume in Italia* 2 [Milan 1964] 313), identifies the types of clothing worn by each figure on the left, including the *veste dottorale* of the third adult figure from the left. The Gozzoli *vita* is dated 1452: A. Padoa Rizzo, *Benozzo Gozzoli, pittore fiorentino* (Florence 1972) 115.

with the spatial organization that had been canonical since the later Duecento. The one clear statement to be made about this painting is that an episcopal palace is represented rising up on the right—perhaps not dissimilar to palaces in some paintings of the Presentation—and that Francis so to speak kneels his way up its stairs into the clerical estate.[179]

Perhaps it was this ruined painting of Squarcione's, with its new organization of space, that inspired the last major Renunciation in Italy, Domenico Ghirlandaio's compositionally brilliant painting in the Sassetti chapel of the church of Santa Trinita in Florence, done about 1485 (fig. 26). No longer belonging to God and the church, a kneeling Francis rather mediates two parts of a *saeculum* that, within a semi-circle, extends from dandy cathedral canons on the right to the jowly laymen on the left. It is full Medicean Florence and Renaissance Italy, where many of the best lay people made one of their sons a priest and, inversely, prelates regularly served as city ambassadors, where chapters and bishops were fulcrums of power for a protonational ruling class.[180]

In this attractively balanced painting the subtle thrust is, uniquely for this theme, from the church toward the laity. Dressed in the clothes of a common man, a sad, almost defeated father moves against the swell, brandishing either Francis's belt or perhaps rather a strap or lash of the kind used in public whippings. But the movement of the prelacy is irresistible, especially since it is seconded by a powerful lay ally. That seemingly maternal figure who pushes with the clergy, empathetically and gently restraining Pietro, may be none other than Pica the mother of Francis, banished for two centuries from the life of her son and husband and now returned. Wearing a brown dress and red cloak, the figure also wears a black headgear, which suggests that like Francis, this person rejects the world. It is, in fact, part of Francis's world of the holy.

Squarcione's and Ghirlandaio's new spatial organization was not the only departure from the tired configuration of past Renunciations. If I were writing another book, I would certainly dwell upon the painting of the renunciation attributed variously to the Netherlandish painters Jan Provost and Jan Gossart (Mabuse) and done about 1520 (fig. 29).[181] Not only is this

179. M. Muraro, "A Cycle of Frescoes by Squarcione in Padua," *Burlington Magazine* 101 (1959) 90. Muraro thinks the figure in back of Francis is Pietro. See also E. Bellinati et al., *Il complesso di S. Francesco Grande in Padova* (Padua 1983).

180. On which see my *Public Life*, chs. 12 and 13. The paintings were commissioned in 1485: see G. Davies, *Ghirlandaio* (New York 1909) 70; E. Borsook and J. Offerhaus identify the backdrop of the renunciation as Geneva; *Francesco Sassetti and Ghirlandaio at Santa Trinita* (Doornspijk 1981) 27.

181. G. van 's-Hertogenbosch attributes the work to Provost (ca. 1520) in the *Lexikon*

the one major northern European painting of the theme. It also seems to be the last Renunciation for centuries.[182] The work is innovative in form and content. It features a bishop and clerk clearly embarrassed by Francis's nakedness, and shows another clerk bringing forth a habit for naked Francis to put on. And most interesting, the painting shows a greedy father who, retrieving Francis's discarded cloak with one hand, is actually pulling Francis's shirt from his back with the other. This painting has a spirit and structure quite different from its Italian antecedents.

But there is definitely no Pica in the Flemish/Dutch painting, and it is the re-emergence of a maternal warmth and compassion in the monumental art of Ghirlandaio that seems to me particularly significant in what is, after all, an almost exclusively Italian pictorial theme. Placed in context, the significance is fourfold. First, from an iconographic point of view, Ghirlandaio's figure recalls the restraining Pica of the Duecento paintings. Second, the Ghirlandaio work may reproduce a renunciation theme *cum* mother that is in fact encountered in minor representations, if not in major ones. Indeed, we found the restraining Pica in book illustrations contemporary with Ghirlandaio (fig. 24). Third, it bears repeating that in 1477 and 1480, on the eve of Ghirlandaio's work, an Italian "translation" of Bonaventure's Life insisted on the mother's centrality to the story of the renunciation.[183]

This painting by Ghirlandaio has one final claim to significance, one perhaps that our biases—but not our eyes—allow us to overlook. Throughout this study, the question of the gender borders that Francis crossed in his conversion has been an important thread in interpreting the paintings. In the early paintings, Francis assumed a position between the protective legs

---

der Christlichen Ikonographie, ed. E. Kirschbaum et al., 6 (Rome 1974) col. 283. B. Kleinschmidt assigns it instead to Jan Gossart (Mabuse), who, incidentally, spent some formative years in Italy: *Sankt Franziskus von Assisi in Kunst und Legende* (M. Gladbach 1911) 11ff. But M. Friedländer (*Die Altniederländerische Malerei* 8–9 [Berlin 1931]) does not mention the painting while describing either painter. Almost nothing is known about it. In 1911, Kleinschmidt said the work was in private possession, of Sutton-Nelthorpe at Scawby Lines, England.

182. This painting had an afterlife in a twentieth-century Chinese watercolor (fig. 30), part of a series illustrating the Life of Francis. The watercolor is a direct quote of the painting. The series was on display at the Walters Gallery Exhibition of 1982, referred to in my Acknowledgments; it was subsequently lost. Thanks to my colleague John Chaffey I know that the "artist's" name is Li T'ien-to, and that the text on the drawing reads: "Returning clothes, Forgiving father." But it is unclear how, where or when Li T'ien-to copied the Flemish/Dutch painting.

183. See above, at note 114. For similar headdresses and skirts on contemporary rural women, see R. Levi-Pisetzky, *Storia del costume* 2 199, 476, 479, and compare the Cinquecento Peruzzi and Giorgione urban women in S. Freedberg, *Painting in Italy, 1500–1600* (Baltimore 1975) 108, 142. For me, Pica's presence as restrainer in contemporary book illustrations makes plausible the argument that it is she playing the same role in Ghirlandaio.

of the bishop, as a dependent who nonetheless seemed to be moving from a sentimental domestic existence among women to the grave world of men in institutions. In later pictures the sense of gender shifts has varied, from a move to asexuality to one in Sassetta from male to female worlds.

Domenico Ghirlandaio's painting proves to be decisively expressive in this matter because he is so direct. Closing out the Italian archive of renunciation scenes, his picture overtly comments on gender movement. For all Francis's humble submission as he kneels before his prelate, he is shown as penetrating into the city of God, with what passes for an erect penis! Ghirlandaio has, so to speak, made Francis erect with the maternal figure's foot! If this maternal figure is actually a male, how this detail should be read is not clear beyond a reasonable doubt. But I do not see how this detail can be present by oversight, as a clumsy mistake.

The same detail can, however, be read from Pica's point of view as well, that is, if the figure is a female. By any reading, the interpretation of this detail must not forget the woman's part—again. It may be her penis! The mother of the saint, a powerful presence in the real history of the renunciation, now finally could be shown passing on her power to her celibate son. Part of the world of the priests, she at once repulses the *saeculum* of her husband and his friends, and penetrates the clergy. She, together with her son, is the instrument, the wherewithal, of the *renovatio ecclesie*.

Why did such a figure of Pica, *mater misericordiosa*, emerge at the end of the Italian series of renunciation pictures, if not certainly in the Ghirlandaio, doubtlessly in the illuminations to which we have referred? Before approaching that question, let me first summarize the pictorial tradition and the story of the renunciation of Francis as a whole. Then we may understand the new social organization whose reproduction Ghirlandaio's Francis so wonderfully mediates.

4
Conclusion

The images of the renunciation of Francis of Assisi that have come down to us were products of corporate artistic practices and of a need to communicate with lay audiences. Those paintings done in the fourteenth and fifteenth centuries also needed to obey an established literary canon. I have tried to show that it was the first two factors that struggled among themselves for supremacy. The written text of the renunciation, though of no little importance, remains last in order of importance in shaping the pictures. The adoption of the Bonaventuran canon did, it is true, have a significant impact on pictorial representations. Yet by the time that written canon was established, artists had developed modes of representing the theme that would unbendingly resist portraying the scene of the renunciation as Bonaventure described it. Inversely, one theme—that of the enraged and violent father at the renunciation—became canonical after Bonaventure even though it had no basis in Bonaventure's *vita*. Indeed the paintings, in some ways do not represent Francis's renunciation at all.

Several corporate or disciplinary traditions deserve to be particularly emphasized. First of all, the practice of conflating different scenes into the representation of the renunciation: by 1300, in the upper church of Assisi, I counted four such moments. Second, the adherence to established composition, most striking the rigorous maintenance of the left-right organization of *saeculum* and clergy from about 1270 till 1450. Third, the painters' mimicking of their predecessors' representations of individuals: I pointed to the repeated presentation of a figure I suggested was originally intended to be Bonaventure, by artists who surely did not know who the figure had initially represented. I pointed as well to the vestigial representation of Francis as prayerful in a pose that originally showed him in ecstasy at San Damiano. Even though the San Damiano scene came to be represented in the *vite* separately, Francis in the renunciation echoed the scene as well.

CONCLUSION

If copying from one's masters was important, no less influential was the need of the individual painters to satisfy their patrons, and the need of both to communicate with their changing audiences. In one regard the pictures show no change, as if the audiences would not accept change or the patrons and artists did not dare to modify tradition: not one picture unequivocally shows father Pietro or Francis as a merchant. More precisely, in no painting is the identifying mark of the merchant, the moneybag, or the money that Francis returned to his father shown to the viewer. While of course everyone understood that Pietro had been a merchant, the scene we see invariably emphasizes generational conflict rather than Francis's rejection of the merchant world. I argued that this conflict of generations glossed the social conflict over money.

Such stasis is not the case as concerns the role of the mother. I noted two trends in that regard. First, Pica altogether, and women in general, retreated to the shadows or even disappeared from major representations of the renunciation in Tuscany once the Bonaventuran tradition was firmly established, to return only in the last major painting of the Quattrocento, that by Ghirlandaio. Second, the mother figure survived during this period in less monumental forms. We found her possibly in an early fifteenth-century lunette in the upper story of a cloister at the Florentine church of Santa Croce in a separate scene of Francis's thrashing by the young, and certainly in late fifteenth-century book illustrations of both the thrashing and the renunciation.

Combining this history of Pica's presence and absence with the invariably nonmercantile representation of Pietro, I hypothesized that the worthier or more visible the medium, the more decorous contemporaries thought the representation should be. This hypothesis is confirmed in literature by the presence in the Italian but not the Latin text of the theme that Pica's estate was central to the struggle between father and son. The hypothesis has its limits, however, as witnessed by the father's violence in pictures—certainly not the most decorous of themes. In major commissions and in the teeth of a Renaissance style that mandated decorum, artists insistently raised the level of violence the father visited on the son.

It seems clear, therefore, that no audience during this period was willing to accept Pietro marked as a merchant, even though most of the sources, including Bonaventure, had insisted on that. Second, it appears evident that Pietro's paternal violence was perhaps the one story-element—though it is not part of the literary account of the renunciation—without which audiences after 1300 would not have been able to identify with the story and representations. Third, the presence of Pica in the early *tavole*, and her later survival in minor representations of the theme, show that contemporaries always knew that the story involved the mother. The underlying story-line after 1300 was, then, the hostile competition of the father with the son for the mother's wealth.

These facts of paternal violence and maternal absence are a key to characterizing the relation of the paintings, directed at a wide audience, to the literary tradition intended for clerical groups. I began by following the first two paintings' relation to a developing literary tradition, and found that the earliest painting was done before Bonaventure, while the second, though probably painted after Bonaventure, described the renunciation in its pre-Bonaventuran form. These two paintings showed a prominent bishop, a nonviolent father, the mother, and in one case a spiteful Francis.

All these *personae* disappeared once Bonaventure's canon was established. Quite as remarkable an evidence of this author's authority, however, was what was now *added* to the painted scene. The Franciscan minister general having said that Francis went into ecstasy at San Damiano, the painter at Gubbio actually showed the ecstatic with his tongue hanging out. Still, such a naturalistic representation did not survive.

I tried then to demonstrate that in the period after 1300, artists modified the Bonaventuran canon to communicate with their audiences. Even as the artist in the upper church of Assisi introduced the (henceforward standard) angry father, so he converted the contorted saint into a properly decorous, merely devotional puppet. The experience of Francis himself at the renunciation became increasingly beside the point in a visual drama that was about structures of dependency and about men's violence in pursuit of the wealth of women.

The picture I have painted of the history of Francis of Assisi's renunciation has distinguished between what Francis actually renounced and what both figural and literary historians had him renounce. Determining that Francis was the son of Pica by her second marriage led to my hypothesis that the battle between father and son actually involved the mother's estate, at least in part. I then documented that argument from the vernacular literary tradition as far back as the mid-fourteenth century, and I suggested that the tradition could have been as old as the story of Francis's renunciation itself.

By a careful analysis of the earliest sources, I hope to have shown that Francis was not predestined to the religious life, as the legends assumed. A sickly young man in his mid-twenties, he had no more associated with lepers before the renunciation than did a talking crucifix lay out his saintly duties for him. Francis was fairly forced into the penitential life by a history of antagonism with his father, and in the short run by his own miscalculation of what, given his legal status, he could and could not do with money.

We have seen further that the struggle between father and son was consonant with the legal customs of the time and the mercantile occupations of both men. The struggle involved not only questions of the taint of ill-gotten goods through usury or unjust pricing, but also—very important—Francis's own sentiments about his merchant occupation and the guilt associated with buying and selling. I argued that these sentiments had a greater impact on his future life than did the peccadillos of his youth.

The Francis of the hagiographers was another matter, and a substantial task of this work has been to unravel the development of the written and painted hagiographic tradition. The hagiographic process of retrojecting such themes as kissing lepers and falling into ecstasy before crucifixes was, paradoxically but not surprisingly, found to have intensified as Francis ceased to be a figure needing propagandizing, as he still was in 1 Celano. As Francis became an image that served the organizational goals of the various Franciscan factions, and the goals of merchant society at large, the stories exploded and were freely manipulated.

But if each author, even each painter, made his own Francis, they all did so within a dynamic context of religious, social, and political history. I isolated the specific themes in the story that proved the most sensitive over time, and traced their development. The position of the bishop, for example, reflected the problem of the immunities of the religious orders from the secular clergy. The question of whether Francis had money when he came before the bishop addressed the immunities of the religious from the secular clergy, but also the disputes of strict and lax groups within the Franciscan order. And the question, important since the time of the order's original rules, of whether future converts to the order should renounce to the poor (that is, in part to the order) or to their relatives in the *saeculum* was one that vitally affected the whole social order.

Certainly the mother's role in the story concerned the whole of society, given the fact that women's property was so important in the actual as distinct from the represented functioning of society. True, until Bonaventure none of the Latin writers mentioned Pica's estate; yet with that writer, her estate was specifically excluded from the story of the renunciation. What are the implications of the fact that Bonaventure had Francis renounce specifically and only his rights to his father's estate? Was Bonaventure merely cultivating the decorous fiction that only men had wealth, or that only male children inherited from male adults? Or was Bonaventure using this story to legitimate other mothers' gifts to their sons in the Franciscan order? I cannot answer that question, but I insist that his mention of a particular parental estate was significant. His innovation, whatever its genesis, highlights the relevance of the mother in a written and visual tradition that soon excluded her from its monuments. From the earliest paintings to the Italian

CONCLUSION 107

text that has Pietro demanding Francis's renunciation of his mother's estate, however, we found proof of her continued participation.

In the early sixteenth century, the artist Franciabigio painted a Marriage of the Virgin for the church of SS. Annunziata in Florence that shows a group of rejected young suitors pummeling the elderly groom Joseph (fig. 27). As Christiane Klapisch-Zuber has shown, the Marriage of Joseph and Mary was a theme used by artists since Giotto to represent men of various ages competing ever more fiercely for young women and their dowries.[184] Our study suggests that the Renunciation of St. Francis was another sacred theme used to represent a comparable conflict of urban cultures: the generational struggle between fathers and sons over women's wealth.

Why did the pictures of both the Marriage of Mary and the Renunciation of St. Francis become ever more violent as time passed? We must look for answers to social developments in peninsular society. I have merely alluded to those developments, for a full integration of our texts and images to social and political developments would be not only another work, but a hazardous undertaking. In his *Feudal Society*, Marc Bloch did not analyze visual materials because, he said, he did not know how.[185] More confident (or foolhardy) in that respect though they may be, modern historians are still aware that developments in the cultural spheres of literature and art have no merely mechanical relation to developments in the social universe. In this work on Francis, I have been further constrained by the paucity of sources and studies for Umbria.

In moving to the Florentine universe, where so many of the Renunciations were painted, I have at least isolated social and political developments relevant to the cultural deposits that have been analyzed. First, I noted a decrease in the legal rights of women during these centuries, coupled with an increase in their formal influence due to the explosion in the size of their dowries. Those large dowries were the more important because of a pattern of marriage ages that insured that women and their wealth would often be moved about from man to man.

Second, I pointed to the question of the relative power of young men over the centuries. That history remains to be written.[186] Scholars are just

184. See the citations in note 165 above.
185. M. Bloch, *Feudal Society* (Chicago 1961) 59-60.
186. Literature on youth within Italian social and political culture includes Trexler, "Ritual in Florence: Adolescence and Salvation in the Renaissance," in C. Trinkaus with H. Oberman, eds., *The Pursuit of Holiness in Late Medieval and Renaissance Religion* (Leiden 1974) 200-264, and for Venice, S. Chojnacki, "Kinship Ties and Young Patricians in Fifteenth-Century Venice," *Renaissance Quarterly* 38 (1985) 240-270 and his "Political Adulthood in Fifteenth-Century Venice," *American Historical Review* 91 (1986) 791-810.

beginning to discover the relevance of generational tensions to Italian history, and research is still at the stage of studying institutions dependent on age and has not yet come to identifying changes over time. Nevertheless I did cite unmistakable changes in the tone of the Florentine narrative sources: a crescendo of paternal fears in the face of aggressive sons, and of resentments by youth of both their fathers and of political systems that tended to exclude them from participation. These are some of the experiential foundations upon which artists, and certainly preachers as well, built up their modes of communicating with their audiences.

Francis's renunciation was but one event in his eventful lifetime. Precisely because Christian merchant societies have evinced such a need for legendary figures of selflessness, some readers may conclude that what Francis did earlier, and especially the absence of providence in that early life, somehow dilutes the quality of what Francis achieved later. Such a conclusion would, however, be mistaken. Recent studies of several cultural heroes have allowed us a richer understanding of them as patriarchs precisely by discovering their humanity at the time of conversion.[187]

Francis the penitent deserves no less, and there is a series of motifs in the story of his renunciation which may, in fact, be viewed as elements of that larger historical self. Perhaps most obvious is that Francis's merchant background, and especially his grappling with the effects of holding money, helps to explain his readiness to describe the religion he founded in mercantile terms of earning souls and paying interest.

But there are more than metaphorical continuities between Francis's renunciations and his later life. Francis did not undress only at the renunciation. If the *vite* are to be believed, he did so often in public, in a type of Jamesian repetition of the original conversion.[188] That is a theme deserving exploration. Again, the biographers' concern with Francis's mother and her place in the story—at times driven home by her omission from the narrative—are part of a larger theme. Not only does Francis teach his brothers that the order needs to adopt and support a mother.[189] Francis himself is represented as a mother—"of many born of his fecundity, not of any [carnal] weakness."[190] This certainly invites reflection on the gender quali-

---

187. As classics I have in mind E. Erikson, *Young Man Luther* (New York 1958), and P. Brown, *Augustine of Hippo* (Berkeley 1967).
188. W. James, *The Varieties of Religious Experience* (New York 1902). Cases of Francis undressing (to clothe the poor) and showing himself "fere nudus" (while preaching) are indexed in *AF*, pp. 746 ("Nudatus") and 748 ("Pauperibus").
189. See above, note 59.
190. "Mulier haec erat Franciscus multorum fecunditate, non factorum mollitie": 2 Celano I, 11.

ties of many pictures of the renunciation, beginning with those that show Francis squeezed between the thighs of the bishop representing Mother Church.

Finally, the fact that the pictures never permit us to see Francis naked, as the written sources say he was, but only with his genitals covered over, deserves exploration. It is worth considering that the pictures, which have often given us more of an inkling of the truth than do the written sources, in the case of Francis conceal his genitalia—marvelous links, in the medieval view, to the physical and animal nature Francis treasured so much.

The legends say Francis talked with the animals. But his more recent biographers have not told how the man of God talked to his sexual part as to an ass, the most despised animal of all. Feeling an erection coming on, says Bonaventure, Francis ripped off his tunic—naked again!—and beat his penis. "Take that, Brother Ass," he yelled; "that's what you're there for, to be scourged like that."[191] If Francis's daring strip before his father was, among other things, a defiant demonstration of youthful virility, as shown so adroitly by Ghirlandaio, what was meant by these later flagellations of that same erect member? The Renunciation of St. Francis may indeed provide entry into the mysteries of Francis's life after he died to his earthly father.

Francis will probably always epitomize the myth of renewal for Christians, but it is the duty of the scholar to discover from the historical context precisely what it is that is dying. As seen in the later half-lives of these themes first broached at Francis's renunciation, that dying context lived on in the new saint. As this work has shown, it is not easy to discover the facts. Yet the alternative to the pursuit is merely to add one more Francis to a tradition of secular and ecclesiastical hagiographies that make us feel good by contradicting our human experiences.

At the end of the period we have studied, even as the Florentines celebrated obtaining Francis of Assisi's tunic as a relic in 1503, a local poet described the mocking of Francis by the townspeople of Assisi. From his lines, we see that Italians still had a strong grasp of what the events surrounding the renunciation meant. Not surprisingly, mother Pica goes unmentioned. Pietro remains the focus. It was wondrous, says the verse, that Francis was so good, considering he was the son of a merchant. And it was edifying in the extreme that a young man would suffer ongoing public humiliation for the sins of his father:

---

191. "Gravis ipsum carnis tentatio apprehendit. Quam ut praesensit castitatis amator, deposita veste, chorda coepit se verberare fortissime: 'Eia,' inquiens, 'frater asine, sic te decet manere, sic subire flagellum' ": *LM*, V, 4.

Someone said, so as to please:
"This is the son of one of our merchants,
who is called Pietro Bernardone,
an evil usurer, rich and unlettered."
Then they came near and boxed his ears,
and they did the same thing several times.
And by Jesus, for two years he was beat up.
Yet no one ever saw him angry.[192]

192. Qualcun dicea per più diligione:
'Quest'è figliuol d'un nostro mercatante
el qual si chiama Pietro Bernardone,
un pessimo usuraio, ricco e 'gnorante.'
Poi s'accostava e davagli un 'recchione;
così feccion più volte simigliante.
E per Iesù, du' anni fu straziato
che uomo alcun non lo vide adirato.

Vita del glorioso santo Francesco da Scesi (Venice? 1525?). This anonymous text was kindly furnished me by Nerida Newbigin. For the reception of the stigmata tunic in Florence, see Trexler, *Public Life* 5.

APPENDIX

The Renunciation in the Primary Lives of Francis of Assisi

1 Celano, ch. VI, paragraphs 13-15 (source: *AF*, X, pp. 13-15).

Factum est autem cum pater eius, familiari causa urgente, aliquantulum a propria discessisset, et vir Dei vinctus in domus ergastulo permaneret, mater eius quae sola domi cum eo remanserat, factum viri sui non probans, blandis sermonibus filium allocuta est. Cumque videret, quod eum a suo proposito revocare non posset, commota sunt materna viscera super eum, et confractis vinculis, liberum cum abire permisit. At ipse gratias omnipotenti Deo referens, ad locum in quo fuerat prius, concitus est reversus—Maiore enim libertate iam utitur, tentationum documentis probatus, et per multiplicia bella imaginem induerat laetiorem; securiorem ex iniuriis receperat animum, et liber ubique pergens, magnanimior incedebat. Revertitur interea pater, et eo non invento, peccata peccatis accumulans, ad convicia uxoris convertitur. Cucurrit deinde ad locum, fremens et perstrepens, ut si eum revocare non posset, saltem de provincia effugaret. Verum quia timor Domini fiducia fortitudinis est, ut audivit carnalem patrem gratiae filius ad se venientem, securus et laetus ultro se obtulit, libera voce clamans se pro nihilo ducere vincula et verbera eius. Insuper attestatur se pro Christi nomine gaudenter mala omnia subiturum.

Videns autem pater, quod ab incepto itinere ipsum revocare non posset, totus ad extorquendam pecuniam instigatur. Desideraverat vir Dei eam in pauperum victu et illius loci aedificiis totam expendere ac praebere; sed qui pecuniam non amabat, nulla de ipsa specie boni decipi potest, et qui nullo ipsius detinebatur affectu ad eius amissionem in aliquo non turbatur. Inventa itaque pecunia, quam maximus terrenorum contemptor et caelestium divitiarum nimis cupidus exquisitor in pulverem et fenestram excusserat, saevientis patris aliquantulum exstinguitur furor, et avaritiae sitis inventionis vapore utcumque restringitur. Ducit eum deinde coram episcopo civitatis, ut in ipsius manibus omnibus eius renuntians facultatibus, omnia redderet quae habebat. Quod non solum ipse non renuit, sed et multum gaudens prompto animo acceleravit facere postulata.

Cumque perductus esset coram episcopo, nec moras patitur nec cunctatur de aliquo, immo nec verba exspectat nec facit, sed continuo, depositis et proiectis omnibus vestimentis, restituit ea patri. Insuper et nec femoralia retinens, totus coram omnibus denudatur. Episcopus vero animum ipsius attendens, fervoremque ac constantiam nimis admirans, protinus exsurrexit et inter brachia sua ipsum recolligens, pallio quo indutus erat contexit eum. Intellexit aperte divinum esse consilium, et facta viri Dei quae praesentialiter viderat, cognovit mysterium continere. Factus est propterea deinceps adiutor eius, et fovens ipsum atque confortans, amplexatus est eum in visceribus charitatis. Ecce iam nudus cum nudo luctatur, et depositis omnibus quae sunt mundi, solius divinae iustitiae memoratur. Studet iam sic propriam contemnere vitam, omnem pro illa sollicitudinem deponendo, ut sibi pauperi pax esset in obsessa via, et solus carnis paries ipsum a divina visione interim separaret.

Julian of Speyer, Vita Sancti Francisci, *ch. I, paragraphs 8-9 (source: AF, X, pp. 339-340).*

Accidit autem die quadam patrem eius a domo causa rei familiaris abscedere, cum mater illius, factum mariti non approbans, blandis filium allocuta sermonibus, sic illum a suo attentabat proposito revocare. Quod cum se non posse conspiceret, materna pietate commota latenter vincula rupit, filioque soluto liberum abire permisit. At ille veluti iam in tentatione probatus, solito securior est effectus, et gratias omnipotenti Domino referens, in magna animi libertate ad locum, in quo prius steterat, est reversus. Quod factum ut domum rediens pater agnovit, iratus uxorem contumeliis lacessivit; nec adhuc cessans, animo post filium effrenato cucurrit. Nitebatur enim ut eum saltem ab illius terrae confinio penitus elongaret, si illum a suo proposito flectere non valeret. Cuius adventui se filius liber et intrepidus offerens, iam patris furiae non cedebat, ut antea fecerat; sed adhuc maiora pati pro Christo gratanter se velle clamabat. Videns igitur pater inflexibilem eius constantiam, demum ad pecuniam convertitur extorquendam; qua, ubi vir sanctus illam proiecerat, inventa pariter et sublata, iam erga filium mitius agere coepit, quia avaritiae sitis paulisper exstincta furorem simul animi temperavit.

Post haec illum ad episcopum loci perduxit, ut ei cuncta coram illo quae habuit redderet, omnesque facultates suas in ipsius manibus resignaret. At ille promptus et hilaris ad hoc ipsum, prius etiam quam postularetur, se offerens, omnia quae habuit indumenta, nec femoralibus quidem retentis, deponens, ea patri restituit; sicque omnino nudus coram omnibus remanens, in mundo se exsulem designavit. Episcopus vero, tantum viri fervorem admirans, nequaquam haec sine nutu divino fieri posse cognovit; et ex tunc illi paternae caritatis affectu paratus assistere, inter brachia sua collectum pallio quo induebatur obtexit. Iam se vir Dei nudus in cruce nudato conformat, iam perfecte consilium de omnibus renuntiandis impleverat, quem a divino contuitu iam nil terrenum, nisi solus carnis paries, separabat.

The Three Companions, ch. VI, sections 18-20 (source: Desbonnets, *TS*, pp. 103-105).

Ipse vero, nec motus verbis nec vinculis aut verberibus fatigatus, patienter omnia portans, ad sanctum propositum exsequendum promptior et validior reddebatur.

Pater namque ipsius recedente a domo causa necessitatis urgente, mater eius quae sola cum illo remanserat, factum viri sui non approbans, blandis sermonibus alloquitur filium. Quem, cum a sancto proposito revocare non posset, commotis eius visceribus super ipsum, confregit vincula eumque liberum abire permisit. At ipse, gratias omnipotenti Deo referens, ad locum ubi fuerat prius revertitur, et maiori libertate utens tanquam daemonum tentationibus probatus et tentationum documentis instructus, recepto animo securiori ex iniuriis, liberior et magnanimior incedebat.

Interea pater revertitur et non invento filio, peccata peccatis accumulans, intorquet convicia in uxorem.

Deinde cucurrit ad palatium communitatis conquerens de filio coram consulibus civitatis postulansque ut pecuniam, quam exspoliata domo asportaverat, facerent sibi reddi. Consules autem videntes eum ita turbatum, Franciscum, ut coram eis compareat, citant sive advocant per praeconem. Qui praeconi respondens dixit se per Dei gratiam iam factum liberum et consulibus amplius non teneri, eo quod esset solius altissimi Dei servus. Consules vero nolentes ei vim facere dixerunt patri: "Ex quo servitium Dei est aggressus, de potestate nostra exivit."

Videns ergo pater quod coram consulibus nihil proficeret, eamdem quaerimoniam proposuit coram episcopo civitatis. Episcopus vero, discretus et sapiens, vocavit eum debito modo, ut compareret super patris quaerimoniam responsurus. Qui respondit nuntio dicens: "Ad dominum episcopum veniam quia est pater et dominus animarum."

Venit igitur ad episcopum et ab ipso cum magno gaudio est receptus. Cui episcopus ait: "Pater tuus est contra te turbatus et scandalizatus valde. Unde, si tu vis Deo servire, redde illi pecuniam quam habes, quae, quoniam forte est de iniustis acquisitis, non vult Deus ut eroges eam in opus ecclesiae, propter peccata patris tui cuius furor mitigabitur ea recepta. Habeas ergo, fili, fiduciam in Domino et viriliter age, nolique timere quia ipse erit adiutor tuus et pro ecclesiae suae opere abundanter tibi necessaria ministrabit."

Surrexit igitur vir Dei, laetus et confortatus in verbis episcopi, et coram ipso portans pecuniam ait illi: "Domine, non tantum pecuniam quae est de rebus suis volo ei reddere gaudenti animo, sed etiam vestimenta." Et intrans cameram episcopi exuit omnia vestimenta sua et, ponens pecuniam super ipsa, coram episcopo et patre aliisque adstantibus, nudus foras exivit et dixit: "Audite omnes et intelligite. Usque modo Petrum Bernardonis vocavi patrem meum, sed, quia Deo servire proposui, reddo illi pecuniam pro qua erat turbatus et omnia vestimenta quae de suis rebus habui, volens amodo dicere: Pater noster qui es in caelis, non pater Petre Bernardonis." Inventus est autem vir Dei tunc cilicium habere ad carnem sub vestibus coloratis.

Surgens ergo pater eius, nimio dolore et furore succensus, accepit denarios et omnia vestimenta. Quae dum portaret ad domum, illi qui ad hoc spectaculum fuerant indignati sunt contra eum, quia nihil de vestimentis filio reliquerat. Super Franciscum vero, pietate commoti, coeperunt fortiter lacrimari.

Episcopus autem, animum viri Dei diligenter attendens atque fervorem et constantiam eius vehementer admirans, ipsum inter brachia sua recollegit, operiens eum pallio suo. Intelligebat enim aperte facta ipsius ex divino esse consilio et agnoscebat ea quae viderat non parvum mysterium continere. Sicque ex tunc factus est eius adiutor, exhortando et fovendo ipsum ac dirigendo et amplexando in visceribus caritatis.

2 Celano, ch. VII, paragraph 12 (source: *AF*, X, p. 138).

Resignat patri pecuniam, quam in opere dictae ecclesiae vir Dei expendisse voluerat, suadente hoc illi episcopo civitatis, viro utique valde pio, eo quod non liceret de male acquisitis aliquid in sacros usus expendere. Audientibus autem, qui convenerant, multis: "Amodo," inquit, "dicam libere: Pater Noster, qui es in caelis, non pater Petrus Bernardonis, cui non solum reddo ecce pecuniam, sed integra vestimenta resigno. Nudus igitur ad Dominum pergam." —O liberalem animum viri, cui solum iam sufficit Christus! Inventus est vir Dei cilicium tunc portare sub vestibus, virtutum exsistentia plus quam apparentia gaudens.

Bonaventure, Legenda Sancti Francisci, ch. II, paragraphs 3–4 (source: Bonaventure, *Opera*, VIII, pp. 508–509).

Post modicum vero tempus, patre a patria discedente, mater eius factum mariti non approbans et inflexibilem filii constantiam emolliri posse non sperans, a vinculis absolutum abire permisit. At ipse, gratias omnipotenti Domino referens, ad locum, in quo prius fuerat, est reversus. Rediens autem pater et eum non inveniens domi, convitiis illatis uxori, fremens cucurrit ad locum, ut, si eum revocare non posset, saltem de provincia effugaret.

Franciscus vero, confortatus a Deo, obvium ultro se obtulit patri furenti, libera voce clamans, se pro nihilo ducere vincula et verbera eius, insuper et contestans, se pro Christi nomine gaudenter mala omnia subiturum. Videns itaque pater, quod eum revocare non posset, ad extorquendam pecuniam se convertit; qua tandem inventa in fenestrula quadam, aliquantulum ipsius mitigatus est furor, avaritiae siti utcumque per haustum pecuniae temperata.

Tentabat deinde pater carnis filium gratiae pecunia iam nudatum ducere coram episcopo civitatis, ut in ipsius manibus facultatibus renuntiaret paternis et omnia redderet, quae habebat. Ad quod faciendum se promptum exhibuit verus paupertatis amator, perveniensque coram episcopo, nec moras patitur nec cunctatur de aliquo nec verba exspectat nec facit; sed continuo depositis omnibus vestimentis, restituit ea patri. Inventus est autem tunc vir Dei cilicium habere ad carnem sub vestibus delicatis. Insuper ex admirando fervore spiritu ebrius, reiectis etiam femoralibus, totus coram omnibus denudatur, dicens ad patrem: "Usque nunc vocavi te patrem in terris, amodo autem secure dicere possum: Pater noster, qui es in caelis, apud quem omnem thesaurum reposui et omnem spei fiduciam collocavi." Hoc cernens episcopus et admirans tam excedentem in viro Dei fervorem, protinus exsurrexit et inter brachia sua illum cum fletu recolligens, uti erat vir pius et bonus, pallio, quo erat amictus, operuit, praecipiens suis, ut aliquid sibi darent ad membra corporis contegenda; oblatus est autem ei mantellus pauper et vilis cuiusdam agricolae servientis episcopi. Quem ipse gratanter suscipiens, cum caemento, quod sibi occurrit, ad modum crucis manu propria consignavit, operimentum formans ex eo crucifixi hominis et pauperis seminudi. Sic igitur servus Regis altissimi nudus relictus est, ut nudum sequeretur crucifixum Dominum, quem amabat; sic utique cruce munitus, ut animam suam ligno salutis committeret, per quod de mundi naufragio salvus exiret.

Bibliography of Works Cited

1. PRIMARY SOURCES: LIVES OF FRANCIS

Anonymous:

    Legenda Monacensis Sancti Francisci, in *Analecta Franciscana*, 10. 694–719.

    Legend of Perugia, in Habig, *St. Francis*, 957–1101.

Bonaventure of Bagnoregio:

  (Latin):

    Legenda maior beati Francisci a Sancto Bonaventura edita et ab ecclesia approbata ([Paris]: *pro Symone vostre*, 1507).

    Aurea legenda maior beati Francisci, composita per sanctum Bonaventuram (Pavia: Iacob de Burgho Francho, 1508).

    Aurea legenda, composita per sanctum Bonaventuram (Florence: Giunti, 1509).

    Aurea legenda maior beati Francisci, composita per sanctum Bonaventuram . . . (Florence: Piero Soderini, 1509).

    Legenda maior, in *Opera omnia* 8 (Quaracchi 1898) 504–549.

    Legenda minor, in *Opera omnia* 8 (Quaracchi 1898) 565–579.

  (Italian):

    Incomenza la vita del glorioso seraphico padre meser San Francesco compilata per il reverendissimo padre et doctore eximio meser Bonaventura cardinale . . . (Milan: mgr. Antonio Zaroto da Parma, 6 February 1477).

    Incomenza la vita del glorioso seraphico padre meser San Francesco compilata per il reverendissimo padre et doctore eximio meser Bonaventura cardinale . . . (Milan: messer Philippo da Lavognia, 15 January 1480).

Vita et costumi del glorioso santo Francesco composto per S. Bonaventura (Venice: transl. by a devout friend of Michel Tramezino, 1557).

Vita . . . nuovamente tradotta in lingua volgare . . . (Venice: Giunti, 1582).

Vita . . . corretta nuovamente e purgata da molti errori (Venice: Zaltieri, 1616).

Manni, Domenico, ed. *Vite di alcuni santi, scritte nel buon secolo della lingua toscana* 4 (Florence 1735) (*Delle vite de' santi* 4).

Vite de' santi padri di Frate Domenico Cavalca, colle vite di alcuni altri santi, ed. Bartolomeo Sorio and A. Racheli (Trieste 1858).

Vita S. Francesco a divo Bonaventura composita. Vita di S. Francesco di Assisi volgarizzata da Fra Domenico Cavalca, ed. Leopoldo Amoni (Rome 1880).

(German):

Die Legend des heyligen vatters Francisci. Nach der beschreybung des Engelischen [!] *Lerers Bonaventure* (Nuremberg: H. Höltzel, 1512).

(English):

Bonaventure: The Soul's Journey into God, The Tree of Life, The Life of St. Francis (New York 1978), ed. and trans. Ewert Cousins, preface by Ignatius Brady.

Jacopo da Voragine:

"Vita S. Francisci," in *Analecta Franciscana* 10. 681–693.

Julian of Speyer:

Vita S. Francisci, in *Analecta Franciscana* 10. 333–371.

Thomas of Celano:

Legenda S. Francisci Assisiensis, in *Analecta Franciscana* 10. 1–268 (1 and 2 Celano).

Vita di S. Francesco d'Assisi e Trattato dei Miracoli, intro. Fausta Casolini (Assisi 1982).

Three Companions:

"*Legenda S. Francisci Assisiensis*," ed. Giuseppe Abate, *Miscellanea Francescana* 39 (1939) 375–432.

"*Legenda trium sociorum*," ed. Michele Faloci Pulignani, *Miscellanea francescana di storia, di lettere, di arti* 7 (1878) 81–107.

"*Legenda trium sociorum*, Edition Critique," ed. Théophile Desbonnets, *Archivum Franciscanum Historicum* 67 (1974) 38–134.

Leggenda di San Francesco d'Ascesi scritta dalli suoi compagni che tutt'hora conversavano con lui, ed. Stanislao Melchiorri (Recanati 1856).

2. OTHER PRIMARY SOURCES

Alighieri, Dante. *Commedia Divina*: "Paradiso," canto XI.
Analecta Franciscana 3 and 10 (Quaracchi 1897, 1926–1941).
Bartholomeus de Pisa. *De conformitate vitae beati Francisci ad vitam domini Jesu*, (2 vols. Quaracchi 1906–1912) (*AF*, 4–5).
Bughetti, Benvenuto. "Una parziale nuova traduzione degli *Actus* accopiata ad alcuni capitoli dei *Fioretti*," *Archivum Franciscanum Historicum* 21 (1928) 515–552.
Cenci, Cesare, ed. *Documentazione di vita assisana, 1300–1530*, 1 (Grottaferrata 1974).
Esser, Kajetan, ed. *Die Opuscula des heiligen Franziskus von Assisi. Neue textkritische Edition* (Grottaferrata 1976).
Fierens, Alphonse, ed. "La question franciscaine. Le ms. II. 2326 de la bibliothèque royale de Belgique," *Revue d'histoire ecclésiastique* 8 (1907) 57–80, 286–311, 498–513.
Flood, David, ed. *Peter Olivi's Rule Commentary* (Wiesbaden 1972).
Habig, Marion A., ed. *St. Francis of Assisi. Writings and Early Biographies* (Chicago 1973).
Pierozzi, Antoninus. *Summa maior* 2 (Paris 1518).
Roger of Wendover. *The Flowers of History* 2 (London 1887).
Statuta magnifice civitatis Assisi (Perugia 1534–1543).
Velluti, Donato, *La cronica domestica di messer D.V., scritta fra il 1367 e il 1370, con le addizioni di Paolo Velluti, scritte fra il 1555 e il 1560*, ed. I. Del Lungo and G. Volpi (Florence 1914).
Vita del glorioso santo Francesco da Scesi (Venice? 1525?).
Zaccaria, Giuseppe. "Diario storico della basilica e sacro convento di S. Francesco in Assisi (1220–1927)," *Miscellanea Francescana* 63 (1963) 75–120, 290–361.

3. SECONDARY SOURCES

Abate, Giuseppe. "Storia e leggenda intorno alla nascita di S. Francesco d'Assisi," *Miscellanea Francescana* 49 (1949) 350–374.
Attal, Francesco Salvatore. *S. Francesco d'Assisi* (Padua 1947).
Baccheschi, Edi. *The Complete Paintings of Giotto* (New York 1966).
Baldwin, John W. *Masters, Princes, and Merchants: The Social Views of Peter the Chanter and His Circle* (2 vols. Princeton 1970).
———. "The Medieval Theories of the Just Price: Romanists, Canonists, and Theologians in the Twelfth and Thirteenth Centuries," *Transactions of the American Philosophical Society* n.s. 49 pt. 4 (1959) 1–80.
Balthazar, Karl. *Geschichte des Armutsstreites im Franziskanerorden bis zum Konzil von Vienne* (Münster 1911).

Beckwith, John. *Early Medieval Art* (New York 1964).
Bellinati, E., et al. *Il complesso di S. Francesco Grande in Padova* (Padua 1983).
Bellomo, Manlio. *La condizione giuridica della donna in Italia. Vicende antiche e moderne* (Turin 1970).
_____. "Emancipazione (diritto intermedio)," in *Enciclopedia del diritto* 14 (Milan 1965) 809–818.
_____. *Problemi di diritto familiare nell'età dei comuni. Beni paterni e "pars filii"* (Milan 1968).
_____. *Profili della famiglia italiana nell'età dei comuni* (Catania 1975).
_____. *I rapporti patrimoniali tra coniugi. Contributo alla storia della famiglia medievale* (Rome 1961).
_____. *Ricerche sui rapporti patrimoniali tra coniugi* (Rome 1961).
Belting, Hans. *Die Oberkirche von San Francesco in Assisi* (Berlin 1977).
Berenson, Bernard. *Italian Pictures of the Renaissance: Venetian School* 1 (London n.d.).
Bernards, Matthäus. "Nudus nudum Christum sequi," *Wissenschaft und Weisheit* 14 (1951) 148–151.
Bihl, Michael. "De nomine S. Francisci," *Archivum Franciscanum Historicum* 19 (1919) 469–529.
Bloch, Marc. *Feudal Society* (Chicago 1961).
Blume, Dieter. *Wandmalerei als Ordenspropaganda. Bildprogramme im Chorbereich Franziskanischer Konvente Italiens bis zur Mitte des 14. Jahrhunderts* (Worms 1983).
Bologna, Ferdinando. *I Pittori alla Corte Angioina di Napoli* (Rome 1969).
Borsook, Eve. *The Mural Painters of Tuscany* (Oxford 1980).
Borsook, Eve, and Johannes Offerhaus. *Francesco Sassetti and Ghirlandaio at Santa Trinita* (Doornspijk 1981).
Boskovits, Miklós. "Celebrazioni dell' VIII centenario della nascita di S. Francesco. Studi recenti sulla Basilica di Assisi," *Arte Cristiana* n.s. 71 (1983) 203–214.
Bracaloni, Leone. "Assisi medioevale. Studio storico-topografico," *Archivum Franciscanum Historicum* 7 (1914) 1–19.
_____. "Casa, casato e stemma di S. Francesco," *Collectanea Franciscana* 2 (1932) 520–534; 3 (1933) 81–101.
_____. *La chiesa nuova di S. Francesco converso, casa paterna del Santo in Assisi* (Todi 1943).
Brady, Ignatius. "The Authenticity of Two Sermons of Saint Bonaventure," *Franciscan Studies* 28 (1968) 4–26.
_____. "St. Bonaventure's Sermons on St. Francis," *Franziskanische Studien* 58 (1976) 129–141.
Brentano, Robert. *Two Churches: England and Italy in the Thirteenth Century* (Princeton 1968).
Brown, Peter R. L. *Augustine of Hippo* (Berkeley 1967).
_____. *The Cult of the Saints* (Chicago 1981).
_____. *Society and the Holy in Late Antiquity* (Berkeley 1982).

Bullough, Vern L. "Transvestites in the Middle Ages," *The American Journal of Sociology* 79 (1974) 1381–1394.
Cahier, Charles. *Caractéristiques des saints dans l'art populaire* (Paris 1867).
Cannon, Joanna. "Dating the Frescoes by the Maestro di S. Francesco at Assisi," *Burlington Magazine* 124 (1982) 65–69.
Casagrande, Giovanna. "Penitenti e Disciplinati a Perugia e loro rapporti con gli Ordini Mendicanti," *Mélanges de l'Ecole française de Rome. Moyen Age, Temps Modernes* 89 (1977) 711–721.
Chastel, André. *Italian Art* (New York 1963).
Chojnacki, Stanley. "Dowries and Kinsmen in Early Renaissance Venice," *Journal of Interdisciplinary History* 5 (1975) 571–600.
———. "Kinship Ties and Young Patricians in Fifteenth-Century Venice," *Renaissance Quarterly* 38 (1985) 240–270.
———. "Patrician Women in Early Renaissance Venice," *Studies in the Renaissance* 21 (1974) 176–203.
———. "Political Adulthood in Fifteenth-Century Venice," *American Historical Review* 91 (1986) 176–203.
Cole, Bruce. *Giotto and Florentine Painting, 1280–1375* (New York 1976).
Cook, William. *The Early Images of St. Francis in Italian Painting*, forthcoming.
Da Clusone, Vito. "Quando ebbe la tonsura S. Francesco d'Assisi?", *Italia Francescana* 9 (1934) 15–28.
Davidsohn, Robert. *Storia di Firenze* 2 (Florence 1956).
Davies, Gerald S. *Ghirlandaio* (New York 1909).
Davis, Natalie Zemon. *Society and Culture in Early Modern France* (Stanford 1975).
De Beer, François. *La conversion de saint François selon son premier biographe Thomas de Celano* (Paris 1963).
Delcorno, Carlo. "Cavalca, Domenico," in *Dizionario biografico degli Italiani* 22 (Rome 1979) 577–586.
Dick, Willibrord-Christian van. "La representation de saint François d'Assise dans les écrits des Spirituels," in *Franciscains d'Oc. Les Spirituels ca. 1280-1324* (Fanjeaux 1975) 203–230.
Donati, Pier Paolo. *Taddeo Gaddi* (Florence 1966).
Du Cange, Charles Du Fresne. *Glossarium mediae et infimae latinitatis* 2 (Paris 1937).
Eberle, Luke, ed. *The Rule of the Master* (Kalamazoo 1977).
Epstein, Stephen. *Wills and Wealth in Medieval Genoa, 1150–1250* (Cambridge, Mass. 1984).
Erikson, Erik H. *Young Man Luther* (New York 1958).
Esser, Kajetan. *Origins of the Franciscan Order* (Chicago 1970).
Feilzer, Heinrich. *Jugend in der Mittelalterlichen Ständegesellschaft* (Vienna 1971).
Fleming, John H. *From Bonaventure to Bellini: An Essay in Franciscan Exegesis* (Princeton 1982).
Fortini, Arnaldo. *Assisi nel Medio Evo* (Rome 1940).
———. *Nova vita di S. Francesco* (4 vols. Assisi 1959).
Fortini, Gemma. *Francesco d'Assisi Ebreo?* (Assisi 1978).

Francis: Brother of the Universe (New York: Marvel Comics, 1980).
Freed, John B. *The Friars and German Society in the Thirteenth Century* (Cambridge, Mass. 1977).
Freedberg, S. J. *Painting in Italy, 1500-1600* (Baltimore 1975).
Friedländer, Max J. *Die Altniederländische Malerei* 9 (Berlin 1931).
Fry, Timothy, ed. *RB 1980: The Rule of St. Benedict in Latin and English with notes* (Collegeville 1981).
Gallerati, Paulus. *De renuntiationibus tractatus* (3 vols. Geneva 1678).
Garnier, François. *Le langage de l'image au moyen âge: Signification et symbolique* (Paris 1982).
Godelier, Maurice. *La production des grands hommes* (Paris 1982).
Goffen, Rona. *Spirituality in Conflict: St. Francis and Giotto's Bardi Chapel* (University Park 1988).
Goody, Jack. *The Development of the Family and Marriage in Europe* (Cambridge 1983).
Grabar, André. *Byzantine Painting, History and Critical Study* (Geneva 1953).
Herlihy, David. "Growing Old in the Quattrocento," in P. Stearns, ed., *Old Age in Preindustrial Society* (New York 1982), 104-118.
Herlihy, David, and Christiane Klapisch-Zuber. *Les toscans et leurs familles* (Paris 1978).
Hughes, Diane Owen. "From Brideprice to Dowry in Mediterranean Europe," *Journal of Family History* 3 (1978) 262-296.
James, William. *The Varieties of Religious Experience* (New York 1902).
Javelet, Robert and T. Szabo. "Extase," *Dictionnaire de Spiritualité* 4, pt. 2 (Paris 1961), cols. 2116-2126.
Kaftal, George. *Iconography of the Saints in the Painting of North east Italy* (Florence 1978).
Kantorowicz, Ernst. *The King's Two Bodies* (Princeton 1957).
Kirshner, Julius, with Jacques Pluss. "Two Fourteenth-Century Opinions on Dowries, Paraphernalia and Non-Dotal Goods," *Bulletin of Medieval Canon Law* n.s. 9 (1979) 65-77.
Klapisch-Zuber, Christiane. "La femme et le lignage florentin (XIVe-XVIe siècles)," in Trexler, *Persons in Groups* 141-153.
———. *Women, Family and Ritual in Renaissance Italy* (Chicago 1985).
Klapisch-Zuber, Christiane and Philip Braunstein. "Florence et Venice. Les rituels publics à l'époque de la Renaissance," *Annales E.S.C.* 38 (1983) 1110-1124.
Kleinschmidt, Beda. *Sankt Franziskus von Assisi in Kunst und Legende* (Münster Gladbach 1911).
Kuehn, Thomas. *Emancipation in Late Medieval Florence* (New Brunswick 1982).
———. "Some Ambiguities of Female Inheritance Ideology in the Renaissance," *Continuity and Change* 2 (1987) 11-36.
———. "Women, Marriage, and *Patria Potestas* in Late Medieval Florence," *Tijdschrift voor Rechtsgeschiedenis* 49 (1981) 127-147.

Kuttner, Stephan. *Kanonistische Schuldlehre von Gratian bis auf die Dekretalen Gregors IX* (Vatican City 1935).
Labalme, Patricia, ed. *Beyond Their Sex: Learned Women of the European Past* (New York 1980).
Ladis, Andrew. *Taddeo Gaddi: Critical Reappraisal and Catalogue Raisonné* (Columbia, Mo. 1982).
Ladner, Gerhard B. *Images and Ideas in the Middle Ages* (2 vols. Rome 1983-1985).
Lambert, Malcolm D. *Franciscan Poverty* (London 1961).
La Roncière, Charles M. de, "L'Influence des franciscains dans la campagne de Florence au XIVe siècle (1280-1360)," *Mélanges de l'École française de Rome. Moyen age. Temps modernes* 87 (1975) 27-103.
Laski, Marghanita. *Ecstasy: A Study of Some Secular and Religious Experiences* (Bloomington 1961).
Le Goff, Jacques. *Genio del Medio Evo* (Milan 1959).
Levi-Pisetzky, Rosita. *Storia del costume in Italia* 2 (Milan 1964).
Lewis, I. M. *Ecstatic Religion* (Baltimore 1971).
Little, Lester K. *Religious Poverty and the Profit Economy in Medieval Europe* (Ithaca 1978).
––––––. "Pride Goes before Avarice: Social Change and the Vices in Latin Christendom," *American Historical Review* 76 (1971) 16-49.
Lynch, Joseph H. *Simoniacal Entry into Religious Life from 1000 to 1260* (Columbus 1976).
Manselli, Raoul. "Bonaventura da Bagnoregio," in *Dizionario biografico degli Italiani* 11 (Rome 1969) 612-619.
––––––. *S. Francesco d'Assisi* (Rome 1980).
Marcucci, Luisa. *I dipinti toscani del secolo XIII* (Rome 1958).
Marle, Raimond van. *The Development of the Italian Schools of Painting* 5 (The Hague 1925).
Maurer, Emil. *Das Kloster Königsfelden* (*Die Kunstdenkmäler des Kantons Aargau* 3) (Basel 1954).
Merriman, Mina Pajes. "A Case of Royal Rage: Ambrogio Lorenzetti's Siena Fresco of S. Louis of Toulouse." (unpublished paper).
Miccoli, Giovanni. "La 'conversione' di san Francesco secondo Tommaso da Celano," *Studi medievali*, 3rd ser. 5 (1964) 775-792.
Mockler, Anthony. "Pietro Bernardone: An Unorthodox Character," in Roy M. Gasnick, ed., *The Francis Book* (New York 1980) 29-31.
Molho, Anthony. "L'amministrazione del debito pubblico a Firenze nel quindicesimo secolo," in *I ceti dirigenti nella Toscana del Quattrocento* (Florence 1986) 191-207.
––––––. "Female Religious Professions in Late Medieval Florence" (forthcoming).
Moorman, John. *A History of the Franciscan Order from its Origins to the Year 1517* (Oxford 1968).
––––––. *The Sources for the Life of St. Francis of Assisi* (Manchester 1940).

Motolinía, Toribio. *Memoriales e Historia de los Indios de la Nueva España* (Madrid 1970).
Munn, Nancy. *Walbiri Iconography* (Ithaca 1973).
Muraro, Michelangelo. "A Cycle of Frescoes by Squarcione in Padua," *Burlington Magazine* 101 (1959) 89-96.
―――. *Paolo da Venezia* (University Park 1970).
Muzzey, David S. *The Spiritual Franciscans* (New York 1907).
Noonan, John T., Jr. *The Scholastic Analysis of Usury* (Cambridge, Mass. 1957).
Os, H. W. van. "St. Francis of Assisi as a Second Christ in Early Italian Painting," *Simiolus* 7 (1974) 115-132.
Padoa Rizzo, Anna. *Benozzo Gozzoli, pittore fiorentino* (Florence 1972).
Piana, Caelestinus. "La posizione giuridica del terz'ordine della penitenza a Firenze nel secolo XIV," *Archivum Franciscanum Historicum* 50 (1957) 49-73.
Pope-Hennessy, John W. *Sassetta* (London 1939).
Post, Gaines. "Two Notes on Nationalism in the Middle Ages," *Traditio* 9 (1953) 281-320.
Prosdocimi, Luigi. *Il diritto ecclesiastico dello stato di Milano dall'inizio della signoria Viscontea al periodo Tridentino (sec. XIII-XVI)* (Milan 1941).
Rashdall, Hastings. *The Universities of Europe in the Middle Ages* 3 (Oxford 1936).
Ricci, Giovanni. "Naissance du pauvre honteux entre l'histoire des idées et l'histoire sociale," *Annales E.S.C.* 38 (1983) 158-173.
Ruf, Gerhard. *Das Grab des heiligen Franziskus. Die Fresken der Unterkirche von Assisi* (Assisi 1981).
Sabatier, Paul. *Vie de S. François d'Assise* (Paris 1904).
S. Francesco d'Assisi. Documenti e archivi; Chiese e conventi; Storia e arte (3 vols. Florence 1982).
Schlegel, Ursula. "On the Picture Program of the Arena Chapel," in J. Stubblebine, ed., *Giotto: the Arena Chapel Frescoes* (New York 1969) 182-202.
Schultze, Jürgen. "Zur Kunst des 'Franziskusmeisters'," *Wallraf-Richartz Jahrbuch* 25 (1963) 109-150.
's-Hertogenbosch, Gerhard van. "Franz von Assisi," *Lexikon der Christlichen Ikonographie*, ed. E. Kirschbaum et al, 6 (Rome 1974), col. 283.
Smart, Alastair. *The Assisi Problem and the Art of Giotto: A Study of the Legend of St. Francis in the Upper Church of S. Francesco, Assisi* (Oxford 1971).
―――. *The Dawn of Italian Painting, 1250-1400* (Ithaca 1978).
Stubblebine, James H. *Assisi and the Rise of Vernacular Art* (New York 1985).
―――. *Guido da Siena* (Princeton 1964).
Temkin, Owsei. *The Falling Disease* (Baltimore 1971).
Toaff, Ariel. *The Jews in Medieval Assisi, 1305-1487* (Florence 1979).
Trexler, Richard C. "Le célibat à la fin du Moyen Age: Les religieuses de Florence," *Annales E.S.C.*, 27 (1972) 1329-1350.
―――. *The Christian at Prayer: An Illustrated Prayer Manual Attributed to Peter the Chanter (d. 1197)* (Binghamton 1987)
―――. *Church and Community: Studies in the History of Florence and New Spain* (Rome, 1987).

———. "Honor and the Defense of Urban Elites in the Italian Communes," in Frederic C. Jaher, ed., *The Rich, the Well Born, and the Powerful* (Urbana 1973) 64–78.

———. "In Search of Father: The Experience of Abandonment in the Recollections of Giovanni di Pagolo Morelli," *History of Childhood Quarterly* 3 (1975) 225–252.

———. ed. *Persons in Groups: Social Behavior as Identity Formation* (Binghamton 1984).

———. *Public Life in Renaissance Florence* (New York 1980).

———. "Ritual in Florence: Adolescence and Salvation in the Renaissance," in Charles Trinkaus and Heiko Oberman, eds., *The Pursuit of Holiness in Late Medieval and Renaissance Religion* (Leiden 1974) 200–264.

———. "Une table florentine d'espérance de vie," *Annales E.S.C.* 26 (1971) 137–139.

Underhill, Evelyn. *Mysticism* (New York 1961).

Vauchez, André. "Les stigmates de Saint François et leurs détracteurs dans les derniers siècles du moyen âge," *Mélanges d'archéologie et d'histoire* 80 (1968) 595–625.

Vogüé, Adalbert de., ed. *La Règle de Saint Benoit* 6 (Paris 1971).

———. *The Rule of Saint Benedict. A Doctrinal and Spiritual Commentary* (Kalamazoo 1983).

Walker, D. P. *Unclean Spirits* (Philadelphia 1981).

Weinstein, Donald, and Rudolph M. Bell. *Saints and Society: The Two Worlds of Western Christendom, 1000–1700* (Chicago 1982).

White, Lynn, Jr. *Machina Ex Deo: Essays in the Dynamism of Western Culture* (Cambridge, Mass. 1968).

Wirth, Jean. *Luther* (Geneva 1981).

Index

Alberti, Leon Battista, 88
Angelo di Pica, 8–10, 13, 14, 19–29
Anthony of Padua, St., 47
Assisi, 3, 9, 11–12, 15, 18–20, 23, 25, 32–33, 72–73, 91–92, 96–97, 109
—basilica of S. Francesco, 14, 16, 76, 79–93, 96, 98–99, 103, 105
—bishop Guido of, 33–35, 40–43, 48–50, 52, 57–59, 61, 75, 77–79, 81–82, 84, 87, 90, 92–95, 98, 101, 105–106, 109
—church of S. Damiano outside of, 32–35, 39–41, 57, 61, 74–77, 86–87, 89, 91–92, 96–98, 103, 105
Attal, Francesco, 61

Baccheschi, Edi, 91
Bartolus of Saxoferrato, 36
Bell, Rudolf. *See* Weinstein
Bellomo, Manlio, 25, 36
Benedictine Order, 68
Berlinghieri, Bonaventura, 71, 74
Bernardo of Quintavalle, 45–48
Bernardone, grandfather of Francis, 10, 14, 22
Bloch, Marc, 107
Bonaventure of Bagnoregio, 5–6, 39–43, 47–50, 52–56, 58–64, 66, 68–69, 72–76, 79, 82–88, 90–91, 93–96, 98–99, 101, 103–106, 109
Boniscambi, Ugolino, 46
Bourlemont, family of, 11
Brady, Ignatius, 62–63
Buonagrazia, wife of Giovannetto di Angelo di Pica, 14

Cavalca, Domenico, 64
Celano, Tommaso da, 5, 10, 31–49, 53–58, 60–62, 64, 71, 74–77, 79, 84, 86, 95, 106
Ciccolo, 7
Courçon, Robert of, 49

Desbonnets, Théophile, 34
Donati, Pier Paolo, 96

Fidati, Simone de', 64
Florence, 12, 37, 65–68, 72, 88, 94–95, 97–98, 107–109
—church of SS. Annunziata, 107
—church of S. Croce, 64–66, 74, 89, 93–94, 96–98, 104,
—church of S. Trinita, 100
Foligno, 32–34, 36, 38–39, 41, 44, 52–53
Fortini, Arnaldo, 9, 16
Fortini, Gemma, 11, 12
France, 9
Francesca di Ciccolo di Piccardo, 7
Francescolo di Giovannetto di Angelo di Pica, 14, 16, 20–21
Franciabigio, 107
Franciscan Order, 3, 14, 17–18, 32, 38–41, 44–46, 48–49, 53, 58–59, 65–66, 83, 90, 106, 108
—Conventual faction in, 40
—Penitential Order in, 15, 19
—Spiritual faction in, 40–41, 53
Frassin, 11

Gaddi, Taddeo, 83, 96
Germany, 31, 33

128 INDEX

Ghirlandaio, Domenico, 100-102, 104, 109
Giotto di Bordone, 89-91, 93-96, 107
Giovannetto di Angelo di Pica, 14, 16-18, 20-21, 24, 26
Giovanni, father (?) of Pica, 15, 24
Giovannola di Giovannetto di Angelo di Pica, 14, 16
Gossart, Jan (Mabuse), 100
Gozzoli, Benozzo, 91, 99
Grançey, 11
Gregory I, Pope, 11
Gubbio, church of S. Francesco, 73, 76, 79-88, 90-92, 96, 98-99, 105
Guido da Siena, Follower of, 75-79, 91

Herlihy, David, 88

Innocent III, Pope, Dream of, 80, 86-87

Jesus Christ, 1-3, 17, 46, 53, 56
Jews, 12, 19
Joachim of Flore, 41
Joseph and Mary, Marriage of, 94, 107
Justinian, Emperor, 12

Klapisch-Zuber, Christiane, 19, 94, 107
Königsfelden (Switzerland), 94
Kuehn, Thomas, 36-37

Louis d'Anjou, St., 47
Lucca, 12

Manni, Domenico, 64
Manselli, Raoul, 56
Martini, Simone, 80
Mary Virgin, 3
___See also Joseph and Mary
Master of St. Francis, 79
Master of the Bardi St. Francis, 71, 74-79, 88-89, 92, 95
Master of the Franciscan Temperas, 95
Milan, 60, 63
Montefalco, 99

Moriconi, family of, 12
Munich, 50, 58

Ottano (Sardinia), 95

Padua, church of S. Franceso Grande, 99
Paolo da Venezia, 94
Paris, 33, 84
Perugia, 3
Pica, mother of Francis, 3-4, 8-9, 10-14, 18, 21-22, 24-29, 31-32, 59-65, 68, 74-75, 78-79, 84, 88, 94, 98, 100-102, 104-109
Picardinus Francischi domini Pice, 9
Picardy, 11
Piccardo di Angelo di Pica, 13, 14-22, 24-25, 27-28, 48-49
Pietro di Bernardone, 1-4, 7-12, 14, 21-29, 31-36, 38, 41-43, 49-52, 54-55, 57-59, 61-62, 64-67, 74-75, 77-80, 85, 89-95, 97-99, 100-101, 104-107, 109-110
Pisa, 12, 64
Pistoia, 12
Porziuncola, 77
Provence, 11
Provost, Jan, 100

Rieti, 95
Rome, 59
___church of St. John Lateran, 74-75

Sabatier, Paul, 11
San Ginesio (Marches), 72, 90, 96
Sansepolcro, 98
Sassetta (Stefano di Giovanni, called), 98-99
Siena, 77-79, 84, 92, 95
Sixtus IV, Pope, 59-60
Speyer, Julian of, 5, 32-33, 39, 41-42, 56-57, 61-62, 74, 76-77
Spoleto, 3
Squarcione, Francesco, 99-100
Stubblebine, James, 97

Three Companions, 5, 8-10, 24, 33-35, 37-43, 47-58, 60, 62, 73-77, 79, 84, 86, 91, 95

Todi, church of S. Fortunato, 95
Tuscany, 6, 12, 19, 72, 87, 95, 104

Ubaldo d'Alençon, 11
Umbria, 5-6, 19, 72, 83, 87, 90, 107

Venice, 65, 88

Verona, church of S. Fermo Maggiore, 95

Weinstein, Donald, 73
Wendover, Roger of, 42, 63-64

Zanino di Pietro, 95

Fig. 1. Master of the Bardi St. Francis, tempera on wood altarpiece, details of *St. Francis Freed by His Mother* and *The Renunciation of St. Francis*. Florence, Church of S. Croce, Bardi Chapel (Alinari/Art Resource, NY).

Fig. 2. Follower of Guido da Siena, tempera on wood altarpiece, detail of *The Renunciation of St. Francis*. Siena, Pinacoteca (originally in Colle di Val d'Elsa), (Alinari/Art Resouce, NY).

Fig. 3. Master of St. Francis, *The Renunciation of St. Francis,* fresco, lower church. Assisi, Basilica of S. Francesco (Rome: Istituto Centrale per il Restauro, Archivio Fotografico, Neg. n. 7965).

Fig. 4. Anonymous, *The Renunciation of St. Francis*, fresco. Gubbio, Church of S. Francesco, view from south aisle, toward right apse (Courtesy of Dieter Blume).

Fig. 5. (*right*) Anonymous, *The Renunciation of St. Francis*, fresco, detail. Gubbio, Church of S. Francesco, right apse, upper level (Courtesy of Dieter Blume).

Fig. 6. Anonymous, *The Renunciation of St. Francis*, fresco. Gubbio, Church of S. Francesco, right apse, upper level (Courtesy of Dieter Blume).

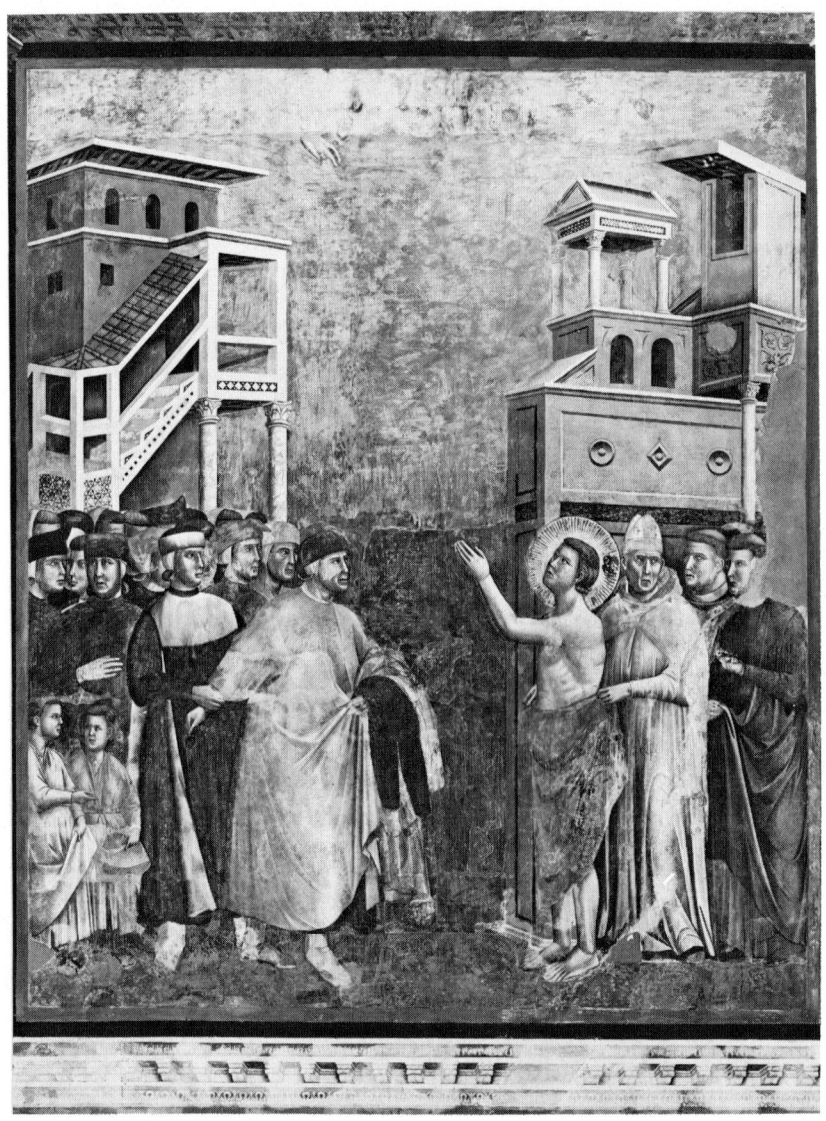

Fig. 7. Assisi Master, *The Renunciation of St. Francis*, fresco. Assisi, Basilica of S. Francesco, upper church (Alinari/Art Resource, NY).

Fig. 8. Giotto, *The Renunciation of St. Francis*, fresco. Florence, Church of S. Croce, Bardi Chapel (Alinari/Art Resource, NY).

Fig. 9. (*above*) Anonymous, *The Renunciation of St. Francis*, stained glass window. Kloster Königsfelden, Switzerland (Courtesy of the Gesellschaft für Schweizerische Kunstgeschichte).

Fig. 10. (*left*) Paolo da Venezia, Polyptych of St. Claire, detail of *The Renunciation of St. Francis*. Venice, Accademia (Gab. fotografico, Soprintendenza ai beni artistici e storici di Venezia).

Fig. 11. Anonymous, *The Renunciation of St. Francis*, fresco. S. Ginesio (Marches), Church of S. Francesco (Courtesy of Dieter Blume).

Fig. 12. Anonymous, *The Renunciation of St. Francis*, fresco. Todi, Church of S. Fortunato (Courtesy of Dieter Blume).

Fig. 13. Anonymous, *The Renunciation of St. Francis*, fresco. Verona, Church of S. Fermo (Courtesy of Dieter Blume).

Fig. 14. Master of the Franciscan Temperas, polyptych altarpiece, detail of *The Renunciation of St. Francis*. Ottana (Sardinia), Cathedral (from F. Bologna, *I pittori alla corte angioina...*).

Fig. 15. Taddeo Gaddi, Reliquary Armadio, detail of *The Renunciation of St. Francis*. Florence, Accademia (Alinari/Art Resource, NY).

Fig. 16. Taddeo Gaddi, *Arbor Vitae*, fresco. Florence, Museo di S. Croce (Alinari/Art Resource, NY).

Fig. 17. Anonymous, *Crucifix Talking to Francis of Assisi*, fresco. Assisi, Church of S. Damiano (Courtesy of James Stubblebine).

Fig. 18. Anonymous, *Pietro di Bernardone Beating Francis of Assisi*, fresco. Assisi, Church of S. Damiano (Courtesy of James Stubblebine).

Fig. 19. *(left, above)* Anonymous, *The Renunciation of St. Francis*, fresco. Florence, Villa Corsini (formerly in lunette, gallery of the First Cloister, Church of S. Croce), (Gab. fotografico, Soprintendenza beni artistici e storici di Firenze).

Fig. 20. *(left, below)* Sassetta, *The Renunciation of St. Francis*. London, National Gallery (formerly in Sansepolcro, Church of S. Francesco), (Courtesy of the Trustees, the National Gallery, London).

Fig. 21. Benozzo Gozzoli, *The Renunciation of St. Francis*, fresco. Montefalco, Church of S. Francesco (Museo Municipale), (Alinari/Art Resource, NY).

Fig. 22. Francesco Squarcione, *The Renunciation of St. Francis*, fresco. Padua, Church of S. Francesco Grande, outer lunette. Modern reconstructive drawing by G. Menin (Courtesy of *The Burlington Magazine*).

Fig. 23. Anonymous, *The Renunciation of St. Francis*, miniature, in Bonaventure, *Legenda maior* (Rome, Museo Francescano, ms. 1266, f. 13v), (Courtesy of the Museo Francescano).

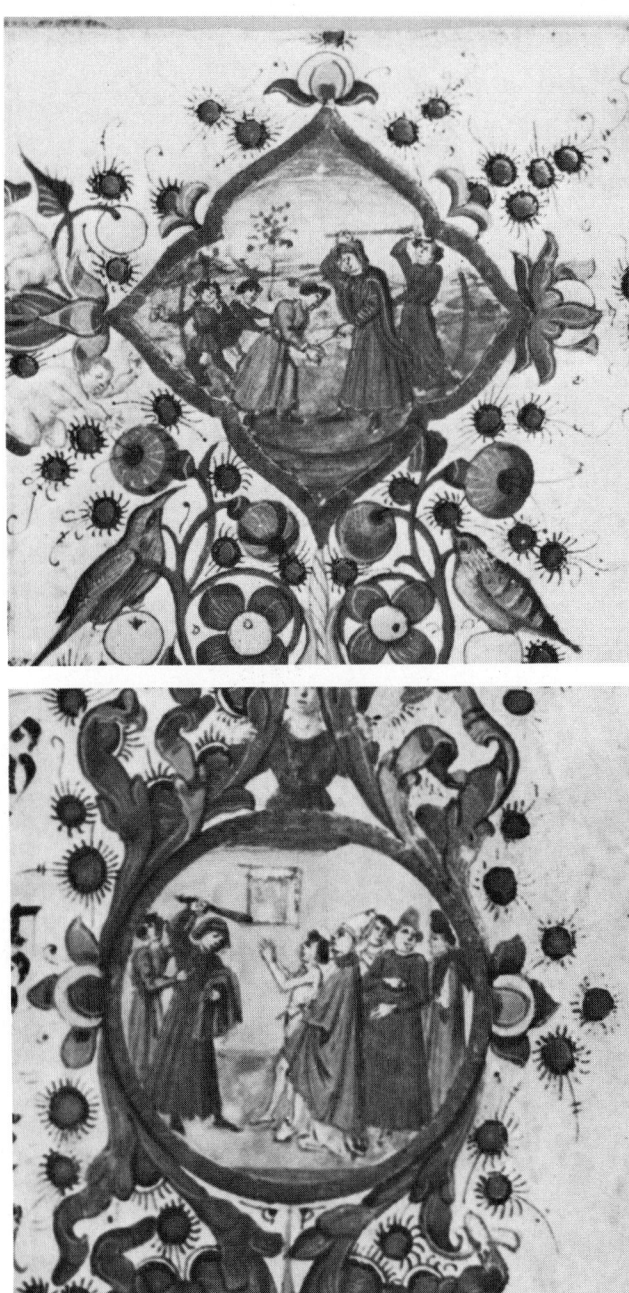

Figs. 24 and 25. Anonymous, *Pietro di Bernardone Beating Francis of Assisi* and *The Renunciation of St. Francis*, miniatures, *Brevarium Minorum* (W. 334), f. 9. Walters Art Gallery (Walters Art Gallery, Baltimore).

Fig. 26. Domenico Ghirlandaio, *The Renunciation of St. Francis*, fresco. Florence, Church of S. Trinita, Sassetti Chapel (Alinari/Art Resource, NY).

Fig. 27. Franciabigio, *Marriage of Mary and Joseph*, Florence, Church of SS. Annunziata (Alinari/Art Resource, NY).

Fig. 28. (*below*) Anonymous, *The Renunciation of St. Francis*, miniature, in *Die Legend des heyligen vatters Francisci. Nach der beschreybung des Engelischen Lerers Bonaventure* (Nuremberg, 1512).

Fig. 29. Jan Provost or Jan Gossart, *The Renunciation of St. Francis,* private collection (England?), (from Kleinschmidt, *S. Franzizkus von Assisi in Kunst*).

Fig. 30. Li T'ien-to, *The Renunciation of St. Francis*, watercolor. China, twentieth century, now lost (Reproduced from a photocopy).

Fig. 31. (*above*) Ernest Wante, *Stultitia crucis* (= *The Renunciation of St. Francis*, oil. Antwerp (from Kleinschmidt, *S. Franzizkus von Assisi in Kunst*).

Fig. 32. (*below*) Cartoon, in R. Gasnick, *Francis. Brother of the Universe* (New York, 1980), (Courtesy, Marvel Comics).

Humana Civilitas

1. *On Pre-Modern Technology and Science: Studies in Honor of Lynn White, jr.*
   Edited by Bert S. Hall and Delno C. West
   1976, pp. vi-233

2. *The King's Progress to Jerusalem: Some Interpretations of David during the Reformation Period and Their Patristic and Medieval Background*
   By Edward A. Gosselin
   1976, pp. x-131; $16.00 (cloth)

3. *The Politics of an Erasmian Lawyer, Vasco de Quiroga*
   By Ross Dealy
   1976, pp. iv-33; $3.90 (paper)

4. *Persian Medical Manuscripts at the University of California, Los Angeles: A Descriptive Catalogue*
   By Lutz Richter-Bernburg
   1978, pp. xxiii-297; $45.00 (cloth)

5. *Rhetoric and Poetic in Thomas More's "Utopia"*
   By Arthur F. Kinney
   1979, pp. vi-36; $7.60 (paper)

6. *Tenth-Century Latinity: Rather of Verona*
   By Peter L. D. Reid
   1981, pp. xiii-158, index; $17.90 (paper)

7. *Ovid's "Metamorphoses": An Index to the 1632 Commentary of George Sandys*
   By Christopher Grose
   1982, pp. xix-154; $28.50 (cloth), $23.50 (paper)

8. *The Discourse of "Il Principe"*
   By Michael McCanles
   1983, pp. xii-142, index; $27.00 (cloth), $20.50 (paper)

9. *Naked before the Father: The Renunciation of Francis of Assisi*
   By Richard C. Trexler
   1989, pp. xiii-129, index